**ANCHOR BOOKS**

UNIQUE RHYMES

Edited by

James Feeke

First published in Great Britain in 2003 by
ANCHOR BOOKS
Remus House,
Coltsfoot Drive,
Peterborough, PE2 9JX
Telephone (01733) 898102

All Rights Reserved

Copyright Contributors 2003

HB ISBN 1 84418 176 6
SB ISBN 1 84418 177 9

FOREWORD

Anchor Books is a small press, established in 1992, with the aim of promoting readable poetry to as wide an audience as possible.

We hope to establish an outlet for writers of poetry who may have struggled to see their work in print.

The poems presented here have been selected from many entries, and as always editing proved to be a difficult task.

I trust this selection will delight and please the authors and all those who enjoy reading poetry.

James Feeke
Editor

CONTENTS

The Photographs Arrived Today	Stan Coombs	1
Taking The A-Road	Lucy Crispin	2
Her Bottom	Andrew L P Clarke	4
Because It's There!	A Odger	5
The Con-Boy	Joan Hands	6
The Watch	Terence Leslie	7
Art Form	Susan Harwood	8
Lottery Of Life	Marie L Westley	9
How Did It All Begin?	K Cox	10
Scale Tarn	Dave Birkinshaw	11
Growing Up	Cyril Skeet	12
York	Debra Sellers	13
Look	Jacqui Bridgen	14
The All-New Pulse Of West Yorkshire	Coleen Bradshaw	16
Youthful Children	Rosemary E Heale	17
Banishing The January Blues	H D Hensman	18
Music	L A Oram	19
Paranoia	C A Bond	20
On The Four Temperaments	Kathy Rawstron	21
Degenerated Memory!	Gary J Finlay	22
Celebrations - A Woman Of Taste	Joseph McGarraghy	23
A 1960s' Child	Janet Greenwood	24
Old Age	A Marten	25
Time For Rhyme	Muriel MacKay	26
The Rose	E B Evans	27
03/03/03	Frank Hansford-Miller	28
Mine	Laura Edwards	30
Amber Rhodes	Rita Robinson	31
Morning Walk	Beryl Mitchell	32
Parade	Yoshi Okumura	33
From Mars	Owen Edwards	34
To Shelley	Angus Sinclair	35
Age Seventy-Three	Patricia Thirlby	36
If Only . . .	Eileen M Lodge	38
The Waters Of Life	Moira Bain	39

Title	Author	Page
Food For Thought	John Booth	40
That Sign	Heather Moore	41
Shadow	Becky Osborne	42
Windmills	Felicity M Greenfields	43
Herald Of Spring	Sheila E Harvey	44
Photo Album (Sonnet)	Olliver Charles	45
A New Beginning	Brenda Brookes	46
Joe MacHaggis	Carolyn Smith	47
Why?	Lydia Barnett	48
A Rhythmic Rhyme	Stella Bush-Payne	49
April's Kiss	V Askew	50
A Spring Moment	Phyllis Yeoman	51
Rosie's Big Day	Lynne Curtis	52
Easy Come, Easy Go	P J Littlefield	53
A Star Named Kirsty	John E Lindsay	54
Old Father Duddleston	Norma Rudge	55
A Prayer For Times Of Worry	Mabel Helen Underwood	56
Where Am I?	Jacqueline Hartnett	57
It's Not Too Late	Jennie Rippon	58
The Princess	Shafkat Alam	60
The Rainbow Trout	Linda M Breeze-Gray	61
Shellfish	H Atkinson	62
Remember Me	Margaret A Leatherbarrow	63
Our Little Angel	Julie Brown	64
Ingenuity	Jim Wedge	65
A Cup Of Tea	Mick Nash	66
The Piper Of Avignon	Barry Jones	67
'Jecano' Unexpected	Reg C H Baggs	68
The Trees Of Christmas	Eileen Burgess	69
Who's A Pretty Girl Then?	Geoff Fenwick	70
For You	Simon McAlear	71
Our House	F G Ward	72
Why?	N M Beddoes	73
The Surprise Gift	Barbara King	74
A Pause For Thought	Richard Lee Nettleton	75
Why?	Marisa Greenaway	76
The Old Oak Tree	Richard & Kathleen Hill	78
My Cat Billy Boy	Sammy Michael Davis	79

Rhymes	June Worsell	80
The Writing Class	George E Jones	81
In A Word	Shirley Johnson	82
Still Faithful	Dorothy Blakeman	83
The Good Partner	M L Oliver	84
It's On The Tip Of My Tongue	Anne Gardiner	85
The Traveller	S Glover	86
Night Of The Big Wind	Terry O'Reilly	87
A Lovely Song To God	Royston Davies	88
The Prisoner	Jondaniel Harris	89
A Walk With Nature	June Melbourn	90
Brief Revelation	Jax Burgess	91
The Old Man	Shirley Wasylyk	92
It's Early Days Yet	V Jean Tyler	93
A September Sunset	Andrew Banks	94
Emma's Snow Poem	Jessica Ruggles, Ruth, Beth & James Allan	95
Trolley Folly	Paddy Jupp	96
A Dream Of Tranquillity	Emma Thackway	97
Parting Company	Trevor Napper	98
Bird Song	Olive Cragg	99
My Part	John Marshall	100
Avebury's Ancient Stones	Joy Morton	101
The Rhymester	Gordon Padgett	102
Hall Porter	Edward Fursdon	103
Good News	Catherine Macdonald	104
Tiger In The Wilderness	Kathleen M Hatton	105
Out Of Season	Di Bagshawe	106
Motion	Terry Lane	107
Broken	Neil Brown	108
What Lies Ahead	Joan Prentice	109
Words	Janet Degnan	110
The Yorkshire Rose	Margaret Marsh	111
The Gypsy	K S Nunn	112
Rhyme And Reason	C S Fricker	113
Dancing With The Devil!	Carol Ann Darling	114
Hostilities	Daf Richards	116
Whiff With Joy	John Birkett	117

Voyage Of Dreams	Diane Howard	118
Samantha (One-Year-Old)	Len Beddow	119
All That Glitters . . .	Michael Alan Fenton	120
Rural And Domestic Bygones	Jo Brookes	121
Brian's Appendicitis	Sandra Kinnear	122
He's Here	Natalie Jagger	123
The Ancient Horseman	J A Brown	124
Farewell To Kephalonia	Pamela J Rolinson	125
Taking His Time	Jamie Barnes	126
A Time For Rhyme	Susan Stuart	127
Scene (Seen) From A Hilltop	Hannah Yates	128
Heaven	Peter Tilson	129
Babylon Stories	Christopher Hayes	130
Winter's Song	Sylvia Connor	132
Street Poetry	Terry Smith	133
Harmony Re-Established	Emma Davey	134
Driving	Nicola Barnes	135
Wraith	Neil Parsons	136
The Wrestler	Ron Bissett	137
Enjoyment Of Poetry	Kathy Buckley	138
All Out!	Rosemary Williams	139
The Last Tram Ride	William J Jones	140
Observation	June Davies	141
Otherwise	Hugh Campbell	142
Yellow Rose	Indy Clark	143
Catnap	M E A Lloyd	144
A Time For Rhyme	Muriel Berry	145
Raindrops	Aves Swanson	146
The Camel	Robert H Quin	147
There Was A Time	B Lamus	148
Wishing	Margaret Rose	149
The Old Orkney Chair	Hamish M Davidson	150
The Man In The Moon	Thomas R Slater	151
Need To Rhyme	Win Barton	152
A Butterfly Flies	Cecil J Lewis	153
Happy Birthday, Mum	Eric E Webb	154
Life Over	Jo Hodson	155
Cat's Breakfast	S R Hawk'sbee	156

Ullswater Lament	John Belcher	157
Beautiful Times	Chris Silvester	158
Home From Greece	Dave Austin	159
A Beautiful Life	P Taylor	160
Phase Days	A A Brown	161
Addict's Spirits	Ivan Daniš	162
Forty Drinks	Steve Glason	164
Mystery Woman	Carrie Thorpe	165

THE PHOTOGRAPHS ARRIVED TODAY

I've received the snapshots today
    Of a recent holiday
Seen on the beach, by the sea
    Are pictures of you and of -
Who is he? It can't be me!
The person that I see must be at least seventy-three
    That can't be me.
There's a picture on the sideboard for everyone to see.
    Now - that is me!
He's maybe a little lighter, eyes a little brighter
    He then, was me
Thankfully, inwardly, I remain as I used to be -
    Relatively.
Seems to me just yesterday first saying precociously
    That I am he,
But youth and maturity hasten into elderly
    For all to see.
Mirrors show emphatic'lly a vague similarity
    'Twixt he and me.
Intrusively photography exposes the reality
    I'm not now he.
One is me at twenty-three, t'other in antiquity,
    They could be me
That image that I see must be at least seventy-three
    That must be me!

Stan Coombs

TAKING THE A-ROAD

Driving back late from love, its flame
bright and steady inside,
I choose against the motorway,
taking instead the gentler ride
of the A-road. Another day
has passed through me: I am becoming calm,
have surrendered myself to night's sure balm.

The car appears to drive itself,
first weaving through the town
which breathes silently the rest sent
to purge its busy-ness, sunk down
in sleep's task of replenishment,
only drunks tacking the longest way home,
floundering through streetlights' pools, lost, alone;

then, little by little, the road
sheds the houses and shops,
reclaiming its own shape, winding
through night fields and woods where trees drop
their leaves, dancing, down through blinding
headlights. These beams create the road ahead,
unfurl it before me; and I am led

onward, rapt, without conscious choice,
my foot light on the gas,
hands lying loosely on the wheel,
accepting the journey. I pass
no other cars; silent, I steal
past silent farms where fields of gleaming cows
are ghostly, still, wrapped in their endless now.

And as I am moved on further
the night reveals her stars,
opening her sky around me,
meeting the light I carry far
inside myself: so deeply free,
so lost into the journeying, I'm bound
to home - so lost, in truth, that I am found.

Lucy Crispin

HER BOTTOM

'Does this make my bum look fat?' is the dare that's laid down
Which way should I go? A smile or a frown?
You see I'm the rabbit in headlights, not sure what to do,
I could end up squashed flat or in a culinary stew.

So with valour and honour I try for a deal
and send back the question, 'Well how do you feel?'
but no, she sees through this and goes for the head.
My face hurts so much that I wish I were dead.

You know, I often wonder why she would seek my opinion
on matters quite clearly not in my dominion,
for each time I know there's a lesson within,
she just likes a fight, she knows I can't win.

The truth is of course that it's beautifully round,
and as bottoms go, it's the best that I've found,
so next time I'll tell her that all is just fine,
and thank the good Lord every ounce of it's mine.

Andrew L P Clarke

BECAUSE IT'S THERE!

The grandeur of a distant peak,
its snow-covered top gleaming white,
sheer walls rising, barren and bleak,
the urge to climb while it's still light.

Circling the loch, I reach the base,
passing through scrub and spartan trees,
climbing fast, the wind in my face,
early obstacles passed with ease.

I find the knife-edged mountain track,
inching my feet along the way,
the ice-cold wall against my back,
reaching the end without delay.

Passing a cairn built years before,
I hurry on, no time to lose,
descending mist makes vision poor,
decision time, now I must choose.

For safety, I should turn back now
and leave it 'til another day,
but I'm so near, I can't allow
this chance to go, no more to say!

The air so thin, my actions slow,
but willpower spurs me up and on,
foot by foot over hard-packed snow,
I reach my goal and stand upon

the highest point and gaze around,
I'm speechless at such scenery,
loath to climb back down to the ground,
just for now, this is all for me.

A Odger

The Con-Boy

He must have a name
Forcing a lock and breaking in
Is quite a delight
For a burglar's whim
No corner is sacrosanct
No witness to claim
And so much to gain
Drawers are opened
The contents are slain
This violation of privacy
It is not the big things that
Matter so much
But the sentimental jewellery
Their quality to touch
And money to find
To feed his criminal mind
He misses the grandfather clock
Too heavy to carry
He cannot tarry
Have to get a getaway quick
So now the locks are on
A miserable fortress is mine
I must remain strong
Never mind, there will be someone else to con!

Joan Hands

THE WATCH

The watch my father gave me
Is laying in a drawer
Although it's eighteen carat gold
I don't wear it anymore
It does not run by battery
Needs winding every day
But sentimental value
Means I won't give it away
In its velvet-lined black box
Forever it will lay.

Terence Leslie

ART FORM

He has this way of looking; like a bird reviewing prey,
The nose hooks down into my heart; transfixed, I have to stay!
Dark eyes alive with promise - resistance loses pace,
His wings beat softly, humming - as I melt into his face.
Oh help - this pounding underneath my skin -
No good; no choice; I'm giving in.

He has this way of looking - like a baby at the breast,
Wide-eyed and innocence projected as he puts you to the test -
'Who me? How could you - I'm wounded to the quick,
Nobody understands me - it makes me feel quite sick,
It's not my fault - it's all the others, I don't mean you any harm,
Come here. Lie down. Let me take your arm'.

He has this way of looking - as if it's all behind the mask,
Your keys won't fit his padded box; they're unequal to the task.
The compulsion of the moment is all that he desires,
Applause for his confection, from the gilded hand of liars,
His truth is lost in echo, beneath the rhetoric and the porn,
It's a brilliant performance, an exquisite
Art form.

Susan Harwood

LOTTERY OF LIFE

In a quest to relieve life's monotony
We put all our faith into the lottery
We all hope for that one big win
More often than not the ticket ends up in the bin
We all get excited
Our hearts leap within
Yet we rarely get back what we put in
You would think by now we all would have learned
The best way to get rich is to have earned
We would like to be handed money on a plate
But as with everything in life, it is all down to fate.

Marie L Westley

How Did It All Begin?

There was a fellow called Adam,
Who addressed his wife as Madam.
She told him that her name was Eve,
But this he did not quite believe.

'I've never heard that name before,
Nor seen it writ on any door.
It's right our names should be the same,
Or they'll all wonder what's our game.

I am Adam, you are Madam,
No one yet has been called Saddam.
Here in Eden, you're my missus,
I'm the one who gives you kisses.'

She said, 'Man, there is no other:
You've no father, I've no mother -
We two are all there is on Earth,
Until we find this thing called birth.'

They tilled their garden, grew fruit trees,
And learned a lot from watching bees.
First came Cain and second Abel -
One each side for their small table.

Now where to send the boys to school?
For one was daft and one a fool.
One to Eton, one to Harrow?
Free-range learning, up in Barrow?

They let the lads themselves decide,
During a weekend break in Ryde.
They both elected for co-ed,
And each asked for a double bed.

So that is how it all began -
The rest of us are Also Ran.

K Cox

SCALE TARN

The Castle Radio DJ Stan Clare owns a cottage called Canal Rest,
He shares it with his girlfriend, the actress Lana Crest,
It is situated on Cart's Lane in the village of Scale Tarn,
Not far from a nightclub called The Farmer's Barn.

Appearing at the nightclub is Lance Star,
He sings, does impressions and plays the guitar,
Lance is a friend of the comedian, Chubby Dino Mace,
They have a joint share in a racehorse called Tarn's Lace.

Also on stage are Carla's Net,
A female folk music quartet,
Sometimes there is Rascal Ten,
A local band of jazzmen.

Coming soon are Los Cantarels,
Spain's answer to The Beatles,
The eldest is Julio and then it's Manuel,
And the youngest are twins, Jose and Miguel.

There is the George Formby impersonator, Luke Lee,
He sings and plays the ukelele.

The acts are introduced by the entertainer, Cat Larsen,
He is the son of the village parson.

On the outskirts of the village is Lant Acres,
And ancestral home of Sir Henry Lant, a local millionaire,
He used to own a factory that made women's underwear.

In a field behind the home they have The Lant Races
Organised by Sir Henry's brother,
This is when children from different schools in the area,
Compete against each other.

The historic city of Arncastle is not far away,
Also the town of Heysmore Bay.

Dave Birkinshaw

GROWING UP

By rhyme or rote we learned to quote
Proverbs or sayings sages wrote.
At school were maxims taught!
To bring to mind from that hidden treasure,
In later life is such a pleasure.
Number tables help us recall
Multiplication we learned at school.

When we start to earn our corn,
From school or higher form;
Future bosses assess knowledge!
As we mature in business lore,
Meet a maiden we adore,
Boss or manager will inform,
Wait until promotion come.

By experience staff mature,
Family increases demand more!
Hence a higher wage is given.
If temptation should arise
To cheat or steal seameth wise;
False accounting may ensue,
Embezzle is the final do.

Audit may uncover fault,
Prosecution finally brought.
Court findings cannot be assessed!
God ordained the higher powers
To punish evil doers;
But praise to those who lawfully
Live their lives quite honestly.

Cyril Skeet

SCALE TARN

The Castle Radio DJ Stan Clare owns a cottage called Canal Rest,
He shares it with his girlfriend, the actress Lana Crest,
It is situated on Cart's Lane in the village of Scale Tarn,
Not far from a nightclub called The Farmer's Barn.

Appearing at the nightclub is Lance Star,
He sings, does impressions and plays the guitar,
Lance is a friend of the comedian, Chubby Dino Mace,
They have a joint share in a racehorse called Tarn's Lace.

Also on stage are Carla's Net,
A female folk music quartet,
Sometimes there is Rascal Ten,
A local band of jazzmen.

Coming soon are Los Cantarels,
Spain's answer to The Beatles,
The eldest is Julio and then it's Manuel,
And the youngest are twins, Jose and Miguel.

There is the George Formby impersonator, Luke Lee,
He sings and plays the ukelele.

The acts are introduced by the entertainer, Cat Larsen,
He is the son of the village parson.

On the outskirts of the village is Lant Acres,
And ancestral home of Sir Henry Lant, a local millionaire,
He used to own a factory that made women's underwear.

In a field behind the home they have The Lant Races
Organised by Sir Henry's brother,
This is when children from different schools in the area,
Compete against each other.

The historic city of Arncastle is not far away,
Also the town of Heysmore Bay.

Dave Birkinshaw

Growing Up

By rhyme or rote we learned to quote
Proverbs or sayings sages wrote.
At school were maxims taught!
To bring to mind from that hidden treasure,
In later life is such a pleasure.
Number tables help us recall
Multiplication we learned at school.

When we start to earn our corn,
From school or higher form;
Future bosses assess knowledge!
As we mature in business lore,
Meet a maiden we adore,
Boss or manager will inform,
Wait until promotion come.

By experience staff mature,
Family increases demand more!
Hence a higher wage is given.
If temptation should arise
To cheat or steal seameth wise;
False accounting may ensue,
Embezzle is the final do.

Audit may uncover fault,
Prosecution finally brought.
Court findings cannot be assessed!
God ordained the higher powers
To punish evil doers;
But praise to those who lawfully
Live their lives quite honestly.

Cyril Skeet

YORK

I am drawn to a place enclosed by stone walls
A mixture of heritage seeing empires fall.
I'm swept along the bridge leading over the Ouse
This watery way advertising cheap city cruise.
The traffic and bustle of roads merged to grey
Blocked out of my thoughts by a bygone day.

The skyline is broken by the Minster so grand
Like a paternal watchdog with a gothic stand.
I walk on the cobbles by houses that meet
Beamed terraces leaning as tourists they greet.
Retracing steps where Vikings once roamed
Recaptured lives in new buildings now homed.

In shops, bars and eateries with menus that range
The air is bombarded with languages strange.
Visitors travelled from lands far and wide
With cameras and street maps are shown by a guide.
As the clocks keep on moving another day is born
Ghostly spirits of Jorvik welcome a new dawn.

Debra Sellers

Look

Next time you're watching telly or driving your fast car
Stop and think for a while
How fortunate you are

Look up to the brightest star, the one we call the sun
For deep within its burning core
Is where all life begun

Look beyond the ocean and awaken to its sight
Aquatic life is beautiful
It's vivid, bold and bright

Look at every bird that flies and watch them build their nests
Chirping tuneful little songs
And think that we are blessed

Look between each blade of grass and every standing tree
See all the budding flowers bloom
And think of them with glee

Look at every creature that lives upon this earth
Wonder at the miracle
Of living and of birth

Look at all the landscapes from the glaciers to the sands
For the future of this wondrous place
Is in our mortal hands

Look at every man and child of every colour and of creed
We turn our backs on suffering
We are consumed by greed

They say that man's intelligent, they are surely lying
Through our misuse and our abuse
This world is slowly dying

Each one of us is guilty, but we don't seem to care
Polluting seas and burning trees
And poisoning the air.

Jacqui Bridgen

THE ALL-NEW PULSE OF WEST YORKSHIRE

Matt and Elisa are the early birds
Where Darren is absurd
Dave is the afternoon man
And Jackie takes over whenever she can

Cain and Hilton are always the first
Kelly makes you laugh till you're ready to burst
Sherwood is here to stay
Where Blay wishes in bed she could lay

The weekend is bound
To be changed around
Saturday morning Darren Kelly is the first on
Then Elisa Hilton starts at ten to do her own thing
And Darren Kelly will no longer sing

Dave Sherwood is also the Sunday morning man
Comes on at eight and leaves at midday
To make way for another DJ
Steve Bailey is then the man
Where Steve makes a new plan

Steve is also the early evening DJ
For lots of great music all of these play
And last but not least is Jackie Blay

Coleen Bradshaw

YOUTHFUL CHILDREN

Children playing all around
Tumbling, falling to the ground.
Happy, smiling, funny faces
Youthful children running races.

Spirits wild and racing free,
Climbing the old oak tree.
Their souls, rise to heights
Taking off in full flight.

Swirling, twirling like a top
Round and round until they stop.
Imagination fills their minds
Singing songs and nursery rhymes.

At last, tucked up in bed
No more stories to be read.
Their batteries, all run down
Silently come to a stop.

Re-charged, ready to go.
'Mum, it's morning.' - 'Oh no!'
The start of a new day
Youthful children shout, 'Hooray.'

Rosemary E Heale

BANISHING THE JANUARY BLUES

Christmas over and what's to show?
No coloured paper or mistletoe,
No sparkling lights around the room
That would brighten up the New Year's gloom.

The glitter has gone with tree to the trash
We are all overweight and short of cash.
Heedless excess of credit cards swipe
Is all that remains of Christmas hype.

Beneath a bitter and snow-laden sky
Those many paying hardships multiply.
Even the tempting January sales
Give lesser cheer in the winter's gales.

Slowly from darkened seasonal gloom
The frailest of survivors come into bloom
Just pushing through the hardest ground
The sweetest snowdrops in clusters found.

These, the harbingers of coming spring,
Show the tenacity that hope can bring,
Displaying such determined resolve
It helps worthless worries to dissolve.

As snowdrops cover the bleak winter's ground
So fresh hopes with spring's vigour abound.

H D Hensman

MUSIC

Listening to songs,
For an hour long,
Listening to every word carefully
As it goes on,
Feeling the music,
Imagining a great party,
Singing out loud in front of
A massive crowd,
Making my family really proud,
At the end of the day I can't
Sing a song,
But there's talent out there that
Will carry on generations long.

L A Oram

Paranoia

Everything I do
I check
Do you too
Or is it just me? Oh heck!

I check I've closed the door
The cooker and hot water are turned off.
That the hamster is shut in and secure
And of milk and bread, we've got enough.

All these things I know we have
Yet still I check and check.
I'm not sure I'm not going mad
- I'll have to check my head!

C A Bond

ON THE FOUR TEMPERAMENTS

Being the boss is this person's aim,
He's gagging for a fight.
Who does he think he is? What is his game?
He's choleric and always right.

Does he seem flighty,
Bent on having fun?
The life and soul of the party?
Then that's the sanguine one.

If conflict and confrontation
Are seen as problematic,
Here's the explanation -
That person is phlegmatic.

Artistic, but with a tidy mind,
And prone to slight depression?
He's melancholy, I think you'll find,
And does things to perfection.

Kathy Rawstron

DEGENERATED MEMORY!

A fear and dread so all consuming,
Steals over me, numerous times each day.
Because of this defunct, degrading memory,
Leading me into misery, anger and dismay.

So freaky and humiliatingly scary,
As to depress my moods in darkness.
Soul destructive - each meeting hairy,
Stripping defences openly into starkness.

Being face to face - unsure - uncertain,
If true or false - right, wrong or right.
Do I speak, actually know this person,
If I'm mistaken, nightmare - what a fright.

Hurtful, annoying and so anti-social,
To pass a friend without a sign.
Look uninterested - in fear I'm wrong,
Because recognition, as usual isn't mine.

Then spend hours feeling mournful,
Depressed depleted, to the point of danger.
Thinking absolution - how to recover,
Looking internally - like at a stranger.

Then hiding as always - here in sanctum,
With fear to go beyond these walls.
Alone to suffer in constant isolation,
Until some other benevolent person calls.

Gary J Finlay

CELEBRATIONS - A WOMAN OF TASTE

I think of her with fondness,
As I taste her Milky Way,
Her Bounty's so delicious
I could suck them every day.

Her Topics were so full of nuts,
They took me by surprise
And her Teasers were so tempting,
Wrapped in innocent disguise.

Mars reminded me of Venus,
With all her complications,
A Truffle of emotions
That make or break relations.

Her Galaxy is rainbow-like
With many hues and lights,
Sometimes as smooth as Caramel,
At others, dark as nights.

I am thankful for her sweetness,
A delightful box of lickers,
Next time I wish to have a treat
I'll think of her nice Snickers.

Joseph McGarraghy

A 1960s' Child

The *fab* and *swinging* sixties! So called permissive age;
A revolutionary time by any given gauge:
When mods and rockers seemed so cool and Teddy Boys did not
And I remember where *I* was when Kennedy was shot.

When Wilson sat in No10 and hanging was still in;
And hair was long and skirts were short and Twiggy was too thin.
And kids went wild at the Fab Four, when they burst on the scene;
And clothes were psychedelic, pink and purple, gold and green.

And hippies came with 'love and peace' and flowers in their hair;
And smoking pot and popping pills and free love everywhere.
And students waved their banners in support of CND;
And Vietnam (the dirty war) was making history.

And Armstrong took just one small step and Aldrin followed soon;
And mankind made a giant leap and landed on the moon.
And many idols rose and fell and fans and groupies pined,
When Rolling Stone blond Brian drowned in 1969.

The toll was great, the price was high, to die became a craze;
And Morrison and Joplin would, and Jim, in purple haze.
And older people were uptight at changes in their nation;
And The Who's song was a symbol of my generation.

And rebels died without a cause, their bodies long since cold.
They got their final wish to die before they could get old.
And fans grow up and life and time and age has tamed the wild;
But life was pretty groovy as a 1960s' child.

Janet Greenwood

OLD AGE

Gone are the days of rushing around,
Or even the occasional run,
So now is the time for sitting about,
Being old isn't really much fun.

My ailments are too many to mention
And my feet are the worst in the street.
Perhaps I should not be complaining,
As I do have a good set of teeth.

The mind is still very active,
Though the memory is not all that good.
What's that you were saying this morning?
Can't recall now, but I know that I should.

My brain still works now and then,
Tho' many muscles have now ceased to function.
Really it's a bit like the railway,
Serious points trouble at Clapham Junction.

So it's do what you can when you can
And a doze in a chair, that's just fine.
Let's hope all the winters are short ones
And the summer's a real summer time.

A Marten

TIME FOR RHYME

I thought the time of rhyme was past,
But it's been revived at last.
So now I'll keep on going,
Although my age may be showing.

At school we had to learn a rhyme,
In a day or two's short time.
It'll keep your mind alert, they say,
I remember every word to this day.

To remember we must help the young,
Teach them poems in their mother tongue.
Then when they're as old as me,
They won't forget where they put the key.

Muriel MacKay

THE ROSE

Her beauty soft as
the rose
ever gentle misted hues
for those alone
she would choose
tempting so is her perfume
close to in every room.

But beneath the
velvet bud
hides the thorn
of fresh drawn blood
for with her love
comes always pain
an ever present
crimson stain.

Her beauty masks
a steel-sharp heart
emotions so cruelly
torn apart
her perfection
just a pose
that mocks the beauty
of the rose.

E B Evans

03/03/03

'What's in a name?' cried Shakespeare, 'That which we call a rose
By any other name would smell as sweet!'

But does this apply to dates?
'September eleven' - say no more, mates!
It conjures up that awful terrorist attack on New York's twin
World Trade Centre Towers
And even William S would have difficulty to link up that tragedy
with other than funeral and remembrance flowers.

For the English it was always 1066 with its Battle of Hastings as a
date to remember,
With Guy Fawkes' November 5 maybe even beating it with its
annual bonfires' ember.
In France it's Bastille Day of 1789, in America it's Independence Day
of July 4, 1776
And it seems that every race and people has their special date,
When a great event happened which changed forever their fate.

But today as I write - 03/03/03 - and for a start in English and American
it means the same,
'The Third of March; or 'March the Third' whichever way it's written,
'03/03/03' throughout the world is still today's true date in the frame,
But it is also unique and it will take a century of years to pass
before a date similar to it will again appear,
For then in two thousand one hundred and three we shall arrive at
another 03/03/03 but
Unfortunately few of us here now are likely to be there to cheer.

In 03/03/03 today as I write, in World Cup Cricket Australia has its old
sporting enemy, England, once again bested
And one of Al-Quaeda's top terrorist planners it is claimed
has been arrested.
But otherwise 03/03/03 will no doubt pass by with only me perhaps
giving it any more than a passing thought.

But I really think the world would be a better place if many more eyes than mine
Alone upon such trivialities their interest did more than just fleetingly get caught.

Frank Hansford-Miller

MINE

Sweet thoughts of you doth fill my mind
With bliss and joy of every kind.

You are my passion and desire,
You set my very heart on fire.

If thou wouldst stand before me now,
I'd swear to you in solemn vow
Forever to be thine alone.
Let me but gaze upon your face,
And as my voice sweet words intone,
Enfold me in your warm embrace -
And I shall watch your lovely face
And I shall love your winsome grace.

Please stay forever in my sight,
Heart of my heart, my pure delight.

Laura Edwards

AMBER RHODES

A   is for Ambition - try always to aim high
M is for Memories you'll collect as time goes by
B   is for Believing in all you want to do
E   is for Exploring and learning something new
R   is for Remembering how much we all love you

R   is for Rhythm that you've already found
H is for Happiness you give to all around
O   is for Obedience you're learning day by day
D is for Development as you run about and play
E   is for Encouragement we'll always give to you
S   is for Success in everything you do

You're Mummy's and Daddy's treasure
You give your sisters and brother great pleasure
We love you more than anyone knows
You're so precious, *Amber Rhodes*.

Rita Robinson

Morning Walk

Bleary the eye as the alarm clock bell rings,
Climb out of bed, dress in my walking things.
Collect my stopwatch, my weights and my hat,
Rush out the door after feeding the cat.
Along the pavement, I get in my stride,
Arms swinging gaily, weights by my side.
Across the road, I look left and right,
Round by the school, it is just getting light.
Watch for the swans as they glide on the lake,
Am I too early, or are they awake?
Familiar faces I meet every day,
Postman and dog walkers, 'Good morning,' they say.
Hurrying on I've a time set to keep,
Passing the houses where people still sleep.
Check on the time, am I keeping up speed?
On the last leg now, see if I need
To go a bit faster, or can I slow down,
Feet and legs aching from pounding the ground.
The cars and the buses make busy the road,
Time to head home now and think in work mode.
Turn the key quickly into the latch,
A very quick breakfast just time to snatch,
A hair wash and bath, make myself clean,
Then back out the door, retrace where I've been!

Beryl Mitchell

PARADE

A duck followed me from supermarket,
I ignored and sped, like a fugitive,
Across the field, over the bridge.

A duckling joined his dad from car park,
A father frowned and spat, like a detective,
Boss the child under the hedge.

The duo followed me to my blanket,
I led the parade and split, like a locomotive,
Caress them behind the fridge.

Yoshi Okumura

FROM MARS

'Twas more than sixty years of Earth
In going round the sun
We first picked up an earthling's tale
Of Martian goings on.
'I'm Olyon, the man from Mars,'
The earthling actor cried,
And told the earthling's Children's Hour
How we, the Martians, tried
To bridge the space 'twixt Mars and Earth,
And how our spacecraft small
Would buzz round Earth and land at will
To see what should befall!
But now I'm old and stay below
Within my rocky home,
Draw water from the deepest cleft -
It's far too cold to roam!
My food I grow in glassy tanks
Which fill my airbag too
For nothing more will grow outside:
An arid desert view.
Last week an earthling probe flashed down
To look for water here;
Good gracious! Are they also short
Of that great gift? Oh dear,
I'll have to wreck this latest probe
To keep them back on Earth
Unless they bring their H^2O
And O_2 'gainst our dearth.
So now they'll think that Olyon
The Man from Mars is dead
And all the spacemen of today
Will stay at home instead!

Owen Edwards

To Shelley
(Written above the Bay of Lerici)

No heavy sadness haunts about the bay
Where last to the broad sea you set your sail
And from Earth's limitations moved away.
You ever spurned the prisons which the frail
And frightened seek, prisons of nation, clan,
Of custom and opinion and of class
And that religion that reduces man.
Your home was ever in the unmeasured mass
Of worlds that move about infinity.
You loved the vistas where you could embrace
Those diverse spirits that air, earth and sea
Contain throughout them, where as in this place
    A sun of deep damask diffuses light
    On hills of olives to begin the night.

Angus Sinclair

AGE SEVENTY-THREE

I was not myself; feeling quite unwell,
My feet and ankles had begun to swell.
I was out of breath and had put on weight,
In fact reaching almost panic state.
I wanted to know what was happening to me,
After all, I was only seventy-three.

After trying the usual things to do,
Like putting my feet up and dieting too,
Cutting out smoking, avoiding hills,
Even trying slimming pills,
In the end there was nothing else to be done
Except to consult the medical one.

An appointment I sort with the utmost haste,
I really didn't have time to waste.
The receptionist fixed me with steely eye,
Huffed and puffed and gave a sigh,
A week tomorrow will have to do,
Unless anything else is worrying you.

It's not an emergency; you are not in pain,
Said she, her feelings very plain.
I was not happy, but had to agree,
Nothing else much was bothering me.
I just wanted to know what was wrong with me;
After all I was only seventy-three.

I returned on the appointed time and day
And to the doctor had my say.
He was a pleasant and cheerful man,
With a winning smile and a lovely tan.
Now roll up your sleeves, he asked of me,
I need to ascertain your BP.

This filled me with trepidation
As I rolled up my sleeve in anticipation.
Doctor, I said, I won't waste your time,
I feel much better, I'm feeling fine.
How old are you? He said to me.
Doctor, I'm only seventy-three.

He felt my ankles and looked at me,
Now get on the scales so that I can see
Oh, my goodness. Dearie me,
Are you sure you are really seventy-three?
He reached for a diet sheet and gave me a smile;
I want you to try this for a while.

Follow this regime and have no fear
All your ills will disappear.
But doctor dear, I said to him,
Is there no short cut to getting thin?
After all, as it is I eat like a bird
And on that I give you my solemn word.

My time is short as you can see,
I have told you my age is seventy-three.
No short cuts for you, he said to me,
Just do as I ask and I guarantee
That way you could live to be ninety-three.

I left the surgery feeling grand,
With a smile on my face, diet sheet in hand.
Tomorrow the big effort I would make,
But for now it's home for tea and ginger cake.
Why not! I deserve it, don't you agree?
I am after all only seventy-three.

Patricia Thirlby

IF ONLY . . .

'Casualty' was good last night,
Trust A & E to get things right.
Young husband, newly wed,
Smashed wedding photo on wife's head.
She fought him back,
Clawed his cheek in three lines black.
Her face was punched and on the floor,
Head down, she bled.
What in God's name had she said?
His mother always turned the other cheek –
All her life an example scared and bleak.
New to the game, son had marked the face,
Thought silly wench should know her place.
His father said he'd gone too far -
You know what women are.
Never mark them where it shows,
That's what every red-blood knows.
Son made humble, contrite advance,
Begging for another chance.
Never again, he said,
So long as we stay wed.
Father couldn't see that it was wrong to hit his wife,
She'd not complained and he'd done it all his life.
Stricken girl just called the law,
Wouldn't take it anymore.
Saw son arrested, sent to jail,
All tearful, trembling, deathly pale.
(Father furious - lover's tiff!
Minor slice of domestic rift.)
If only beaten wives could follow suit,
Violence might never take strong root,
Then sons might learn what's good and bad
And never, ever, copy Dad.

Eileen M Lodge

THE WATERS OF LIFE

The stream began to trickle over the pebbles on the ground
The water wasn't very deep and in it nothing much was to be found.

As it progressed a little further, little fishes did appear
The depth became greater and the water louder you could hear.
The greenery got more luscious, it being nourished more,
The fishes they grew larger and multiplied by the score.

Not only did the depth grow, the width expanded too,
And when you think about it, it's similar to me and you.
As we grow and age in life the richer we become,
The more we carry and give out for ourselves and everyone.
The depth and width grow greater with every inch and mile,
The sun upon the water like an ever friendly smile.

Life is there to be enjoyed and has a purpose too,
Each ripple and each lap uncovers something new.
It doesn't always flow that straight, it meanders now and then,
But it's always up to us to regain ourselves again.

As like life that stream goes on and never has an end,
Each stage that it progresses through the more that it transcends.
It's nice to know we'll do the same, a comfort it can be,
To think that the waters of life are just like you and me.

Moira Bain

FOOD FOR THOUGHT

How to have a good and healthy life.
How often this statement I see
And every time I read those words,
I wonder, if on this planet I should be?

I'm told if you drink this, or eat that,
You'll be bad inside and get fat.
It seems fry-ups, crisps and greasy chips
Shouldn't ever pass my lips.

Cups of coffee, mugs of tea,
These two things are bad for me
And it's made very clear,
Two pints a night is 'two' much beer.

I can't sit outside on a summer's day,
The sun will damage my skin in some way.
Can I smoke when the telly's off?
No, too many fags will make you cough.

I'm no body-builder, that's plain to see,
For inside a gym, you won't find me.
Never lifted weights, I can't go jogging,
Well, maybe it's weight-lifting, carrying the shopping.

Once more I'm wondering if on this earth I should be,
For I drink coffee and mugs of tea,
I'll have fry-ups and a bag of chips
And often beer and crisps pass my lips.

So I'm thinking, if everything I've read is true,
For a good healthy life, there's only one thing to do.
Next time we have a summer's day, indoors I'll stay,
Without a fag *and - slowly - fade - away* . . .

John Booth

THAT SIGN

There was a time when aged about nine,
Being able to write line after line, trying to make it rhyme.
My mother said I was doing fine and all I needed was 'a sign'
        and carried on smoking her favourite Woodbine!

Through the years I had 'that sign' - and the time
To express my feelings, not always easy to define - but mine all mine,
I needed direction and words (all sorts) incentive and inspiration
        to pen my thoughts.

Listening to music, so divine, or enjoying warm sunshine
In New York when spending a dime, or in Virginia on the rail of the
                                                    lonesome pine,
When out dining or reclining with a glass of wine
At New Year, singing Old Lang Syne.

The magic of cruising down the Rhine - sipping lager with a dash
                                                        of lime,
And in France, when picking grapes from the vine - on Sunday
                                      listening to the church bells chime
And even when cleaning dust and grime!

Over 60 years have passed and now I'm in my prime,
Can cross my heart and say I've never committed a crime,
But had a definite fulfilment - I got 'that sign' and I really can
                                              make words rhyme -
Though I will admit - there are times when I whinge and whine.

Heather Moore

Shadow

The inseparable figure by my side,
Exact without definition
My closest lost companion
Lacking feature or impression.

The imprint of my existence
Keeper of hidden speech
No uttered noise or spoken word
No returned smile, or soul to reach.

An insubstantial remnant
Incomplete, empty, unreal
A colourless memory
No heart or warmth to feel.

Becky Osborne

WINDMILLS

Their size and shape may vary,
unchanged their function is.
Relentlessly, the elements they parry
soundless, save for a gentle swish.

Arms, driven by the winds, rotate,
producing power; turning wheels.
Uncaring; unmindful of their fate,
as nature's strength they steal.

Functional in bygone days,
Dutch models, fat and squat.
Though many now just lie in ruins,
as timbers; sheeting; sails rot.

Replaced by turbines, tall and slim,
propellers mounted on a pole.
Nature's harvest they seek to win,
new methods meant to plug a hole.

Green energy's more urgent now,
as harmful gases choke our world.
Man seeks a cure; but's not sure how
so history; a plan unfurled.

Windmills, modern, tall and slim,
herds of them, grazing on the hills.
As man, today, now farms the wind
to plug a hole; yet live as he will!

Felicity M Greenfields

HERALD OF SPRING

Candlemas holy flower, of spring you tell,
Showing us clearly that everything's well,
Spring's on the way! For deep down underground
New life is stirring. Soon spring comes around!
Heart-lifting whiteness in churchyard and dell,
White petals open round green-streaked white bell,
Piercing the ground with your sharp-tipped green leaf.
Welcome sweet snowdrop, of heralds the chief.

Sheila E Harvey

Photo Album (Sonnet)

A moment in time captures your pleasure,
A thousand words define your photograph.
'Tis for me to remember at leisure -
Pictured words in an endless paragraph.
As I turn through the pages that remind,
My favourite pictures are the ones of us.
Then one of you I'm excited to find -
In a field of yellow, and soft focus;
With wild grass lush green and the sky cool blue.
Some are also taken in black and white,
The world is a frame for beautiful you -
How paper captures a wonderful sight.
Some of the images appear so clear,
'Tis just a picture - but you seem so near.

Olliver Charles

A New Beginning

If today was not to your liking,
Just don't start getting depressed.
Good things could be starting tomorrow.
Don't miss out! Get up early and dress.

Get out and about to find what you need,
It could be somewhere out there
And whilst you are busy looking,
You'll be filling your lungs with fresh air!

Greet other searchers with a smile,
Maybe they're sharing your quest,
Even that lonely jogger you'll see
Dashing past - a blur in a vest!

Whilst you are busy searching,
You will witness some beautiful things,
The hue of the sky, the trees and the flowers,
Share the joy of the birds as they sing.

When you have finished your search for today
And if you have not found what you seek,
Take heart! There's a brand new day tomorrow!
In fact, there are seven new days every week!

Brenda Brookes

JOE MACHAGGIS

A Scottish highland cottage stood
At the edge of a highland wood:
White stone walls and windows bare,
A Scottish Highlander lives there -
Joe MacHaggis is his name
(Not akin to haggis fame),
Lonely figure with his sheep:
Shepherd of the moors, to keep
Wealthy lowlanders in meat
And their housedogs at their feet . . .
Poorly clad, MacHaggis dwells
In that cottage, where are smells
Of black peat fresh-cut each dawn
As blackbirds announce new morn,
Of new heather; summer grows a
Royal robe . . .
                  MacHaggis goes
O'er the moors to travel afar
Leaving cottage door ajar,
Never wary of the man
Who in town, steals all he can!
Of such possessions has he none
But with the highland he is one:
This highland wood and highland moor -
Its life and breath come to his door
While city folk, in car and train
No country thought e'er entertain
Of winter snows or autumn rains -
The wealthiest of all domains . . .

Carolyn Smith

WHY?

If you could see what I can see
When I look at you,
You would not need to ask me
Why I love you as I do.
You would see that lovely smile
That brightens every day,
Hear the laughter in your voice
That makes me want to stay
To be with you forever,
No matter what's in store,
For each day will be better
Than the one that's gone before.
I want to spend my life with you
Until the day I die,
If you could see what I can see,
You would not ask me why.

Lydia Barnett

A Rhythmic Rhyme

I think in rhyme and write in rhyme
My pen and I do it all the time!
As one breathes, the energy flows
Words just tumble and on it goes.
Feeling the rhythm like marching feet,
Not the disorder of an army's retreat!

A rhyming poem travels happily,
When in print, the world it will see.
Finding a shelf in a shop or library,
Reaching folk, like you and me.
The communication scans more easily
And simply helps one's memory.

Take a walk and you will find
How words just simply fill your mind.
A rhythmic rhyme flows naturally
With any subject you will agree.
Children's nursery poems have longevity,
So, traditional rhyming is still meant to be.

Stella Bush-Payne

APRIL'S KISS

Winter is a time when Nature slumbers
And days go by and nothing seems to stir.
Living things sleep on in countless numbers,
Resting in their feathers or their fur.
Every bulb and every shoot is waiting,
Waiting for he signal they must heed.
As soon as cold and darkness is abating,
Then they will respond with urgent speed.
What is the call that always makes them stir
And fill all our world with springtime's bliss?
What makes this yearly magic now occur?
It is the gentle touch of April's kiss.

V Askew

A Rhythmic Rhyme

I think in rhyme and write in rhyme
My pen and I do it all the time!
As one breathes, the energy flows
Words just tumble and on it goes.
Feeling the rhythm like marching feet,
Not the disorder of an army's retreat!

A rhyming poem travels happily,
When in print, the world it will see.
Finding a shelf in a shop or library,
Reaching folk, like you and me.
The communication scans more easily
And simply helps one's memory.

Take a walk and you will find
How words just simply fill your mind.
A rhythmic rhyme flows naturally
With any subject you will agree.
Children's nursery poems have longevity,
So, traditional rhyming is still meant to be.

Stella Bush-Payne

APRIL'S KISS

Winter is a time when Nature slumbers
And days go by and nothing seems to stir.
Living things sleep on in countless numbers,
Resting in their feathers or their fur.
Every bulb and every shoot is waiting,
Waiting for he signal they must heed.
As soon as cold and darkness is abating,
Then they will respond with urgent speed.
What is the call that always makes them stir
And fill all our world with springtime's bliss?
What makes this yearly magic now occur?
It is the gentle touch of April's kiss.

V Askew

A Spring Moment

As I wander through the country lanes
I feel my spirits rise,
The air is cool and chilly,
The sun too bright for my eyes.

The trees are showing signs of green,
Buds are breaking through,
Daffodils' yellow faces shine,
Pink blossom bursts anew.

Clear blue skies, sweet scented flowers,
New life does everywhere appear,
Worldly troubles, private griefs
Banished for a moment at least -
All that seemed so dark and drear

Thank God that spring is here!

Phyllis Yeoman

Rosie's Big Day

Travel on the train to the NEC,
Roll out the green carpet, we're ready you see,
People trundling trolleys with dogs caged inside,
All contenders for a Crufts rosette to display with pride.
Is this all worth it, they wonder yet again?
Exhausted by long journeys by car or by train,
As coaches draw up, dogs and exhibitors appear,
I'm only a youngster and I'm trembling with fear,
Strange noises and smells I cannot recognise,
I wish I was home, oh, I just want to hide!
The hustle and bustle and the tannoys as well,
I don't think this is Heaven, more like doggie hell!
Everything here is so unfamiliar to me
With every breed of dog I could hope to see.
We cross the Piazza with its black and white chequered floor,
Then it's out for a wee-wee and now I've sawdust on my paw!
Lifted onto my grooming table where I stand so good,
For a quick wash and brush up cos I'm a Yorkshire Pud!
Until my coat shines glossy, silky textured and fine,
With my straight centre parting and a spirit level top line.
My finishing touch is a neat crimson bow,
Fastened to my topknot, I'm a Yorkshire terrier you know.
Then out in the ring and onto my box,
Standing still and proud, Mum slips me a 'doggie choc,'
The judge walks past with a serious stare in his eye,
Groomed with my antique, silver-backed brush, I'm Mum's joy
                                              and pride.

Although I took part and did my very best,
It was hard for a youngster like me to beat the rest!
Perhaps when I'm older and more used to this place,
I'll win a big silver trophy for Mum's table to grace.
Now home to bed, what a day it has been,
Now a good long rest and in my sleep –
                              About Crufts I can dream!

Lynne Curtis

EASY COME, EASY GO

Chance and opportunity lie at my feet,
As I flit down the sunny-sided street,
Paved with gold, a young man's dream,
Money making is my aim, is my theme,
To grab a piece of the action is my goal,
Mobile's ringing and I'm on a roll,
Investments made, deposits placed,
To a healthy profit I quickly race,
Wheeling and dealing is second nature to me,
It's easy as ABC or 123,
Luck and good fortune are at my side,
On easy street soon I will reside.
Some years later, the smile vanished from my face,
Bright, confident, upwardly mobile me, couldn't hack the pace,
Things began to crumble, my halo teetered and slipped,
My effervescence and bounce along with my wings were clipped,
Can't explain this chasm I've fallen into,
Suddenly my judgement is unsound, I don't know what to do,
My fortune, so easily acquired and earned,
Is falling through my hands as if my fingers were burned,
Things are going wrong that I did not foresee,
The future is looking very bleak for mine and me,
Bankruptcy or foreclosure is the only course,
As I am swept away by this undeniable force,
Hung out to dry, a catastrophe for me, an all time low,
My favourite saying comes back to haunt me: easy come, easy go.

P J Littlefield

A Star Named Kirsty

Across the velvet veil of night,
Amongst the stars all twinkling bright
Is one of gold, a sheer delight,
The birthday gift, a star named Kirsty.
So when you wish upon a star,
Her charm and wit is there to share.

John E Lindsay

OLD FATHER DUDDLESTON

When old Father Duddleston
Sits at the organ,
He thinks of his sports car,
A bright yellow Morgan.
Blackbird has spoken
Is hymn number one,
Green hills far away,
The pace rushes on:
Onward the soldiers,
Step out with despatch,
Time for collection,
Oh where is my cash?
Psalms and responses
In double quick time,
While the bell ringers finish
Their last pealing chime:
Breathless the singers,
Break into a run,
The service is over
Before it's begun!

Norma Rudge

A Prayer For Times Of Worry

When life's tempests overwhelm,
    When our barque of faith is tossed,
Come, Lord Jesus, take the helm,
    Show us hope is never lost!
We can put our trust in You,
    Knowing well that God's own Son
Is our helmsman and our crew
    And through You salvation's won.

Grant that brighter days my dawn
    When our faith has reached the shore,
When anew our hope is born,
    And God's power we doubt no more.
Let us in Creation see
    All that shows His love for man.
He created us to be
    Part of His resplendent plan.

Greens of springtime, when we look
    On the silken sheen of leaves;
Gilded flowers in shady nook -
    Summer's beauty gold achieves;
Autumn's darker, richer browns,
    Show us God His promise keeps
When Earth's energy He crowns,
    Gives us food as winter sleeps.

Rain and sun and sea and land,
    Seasons bringing toil and food,
Day and night are in His hand,
    All created for our good;
Times of darkness and of sun,
    Fear and pleasure, life and breath;
Grant belief, Lord, God's own Son,
    That you vanquished sin and death.

Mabel Helen Underwood

WHERE AM I?

Anywhere the river runs, this is where I'll be.
Running with the water, running wild and free.
Free from all my worries, free from all my woes,
Laughing with the water as on and on it goes.
Rushing with the river, flowing to the sea,
Anywhere the water runs, that's where you'll find me.

Jacqueline Hartnett

It's Not Too Late

It's not too late, it's not too late,
It's not too late to lose some weight.
The time is right to make a start.
Learn to refuse that apple tart.
And all the food that made me fat
Will have to go - just like that.

Weight Watchers will help me, that I know,
If I count points and always go
To all the meetings every week -
My weight will drop - I'll soon look sleek.
So yes, I got my finger out
And joined the programme – without doubt

It was the best thing I could do
To try and lose a stone or two.
The people there were very nice
And I was weighed in just a trice.
I had a newfound determination
To lose this weight or face damnation.

I was told of points and such
And how from little then came much.
I put this info to the test
And found it simple - just the best.
The weeks went on, the weight came off.
Now I no longer wish to scoff.

Pastries, chocolate - without doubt
Are things that I can live without.
Just substitute a Weight Watchers' pud.
They really are so very good
So now there's 3½ stone gone
And all through the months I won't put it on.

I'm so determined - watch this space.
I know my daughter's on my case.
We've got our act together now.
We keep each other on track somehow.
We plan our meals with great precision.
To stay on course is our decision.

So thanks to all the Weight Watchers' team,
We're going to realise our dream
Of losing weight - and so it should,
Show on the scales that we've been good.
So on that happy note of cheer
It's going to be a really good year.

Jennie Rippon

THE PRINCESS

Roses fall on your feet,
Oh! Gorgeous girl so sweet;
Moon fades when you come out,
Leaves turn green, when you open your mouth;

To describe you, only a poet's pen will do,
To marry you, only a prince will woo;
I am pleased to witness your charm,
Your soul can wither all storms;

Blessed your thoughts that are in mind,
Pure your tears, if one can find;
Pleasant your presence, lucky ones get,
To get you ages one waits;

A soft and hearing touch possesses your finger,
Accompanying you goes every danger;
Earth is blessed which has your feet,
I am not lucky, we both can never meet.

Shafkat Alam

THE RAINBOW TROUT

Let me tell you about a fishy tale,
About a little fish with skin so pale,
With no colour, not even a patch,
He really was not much of a catch.
With skin so pale he was so shy
And all the other fish would pass him by
Displaying colours so akin,
His only wish was for a beautiful skin.
But one day he saw wonderful colours in the sky
That made him want to leap and fly.
He leapt and leapt until he was on the trail,
Then he caught a rainbow with his tail.
There within the rainbow he felt a glow,
With every colour that one could now.
All the colours of the rainbow were in his skin without a doubt,
So now everyone called him a beautiful rainbow trout.

Linda M Breeze-Gray

SHELLFISH

Mussels and limpets are neighbours,
Whilst winkles and whelks move around,
But the cockle just lives like a hermit
Buried in sand underground.

H Atkinson

REMEMBER ME

Close your eyes and think of me
I'm in the sky, the earth, the sea,
Look around you at my creation,
Join with me in celebration.
Life is what you put in,
Live together without sin.
Peace on Earth, goodwill to men,
Remember the past and remember when
I came to heal and preach to you,
Yet still I couldn't convince a few.
My life lives on inside you all,
Live together, stand up tall,
Help a neighbour or a friend,
Pick up a phone, or that letter send.
Keep in touch, spread the word,
Remember all the good you've heard.
As Sunday comes my doors are open,
Listen to my words that are spoken.
I'm in the sky, the earth, the sea,
Now say amen and remember me . . .

Margaret A Leatherbarrow

Our Little Angel

We miss you so little girl,
you were our shining light.
When you left and went away
our day turned into night.

You're not so very far away,
in God's care above.
And every day a prayer
is sent to you with love.

We will always love you
as we treasure every smile,
every special little kiss
you gave us all the while.

All those special days are gone,
God let you spend with us.
Take care of our angel, Lord,
in your home above.

Julie Brown

INGENUITY

Erasmus Morgan loved playing the organ
In the church on top of the hill.
The wind blew so rife there was no need for pipes
So Morgan just played at will.
He'd never been trained in music or song,
So he picked it up as he went along.
For the church on the hill was totally red-bricked,
But sadly, now, was derelict.
With the help of his friend Wilson-Cusick,
They produced some virtuosi music.
But how did they do it without an organ?
'It is easy,' replied Erasmus Morgan.
The church itself is full of spaces
In between which the wind always races.
By covering a few with their feet and their hands,
Morgan and Cusick could play like the bands
Of woodwind artistes from Glasgow or Lurgan
And it sounded as good as Canterbury's organ.
Between them they had great co-ordination,
Which was greatly appreciated by a large congregation,
Who sat by their hearths in the valley below
And listened to the music, as the fires did glow.
Knot holes, cracks, gaps in the wall,
Morgan and Cusick could play them all.
For the wind which sometimes ruins the crops,
Provided an alternative to organ-stops.
But one thing is clear for everyone to see,
It's very hard to beat ingenuity.

Jim Wedge

A Cup Of Tea

If you watch 'EastEnders', in every single show,
Someone says, 'I'll put the kettle on
And make a cup of tea.' I don't know why this should be so,
Without that line, the show could not go on.

We have our own opinions
On the relevance of tea,
I'd sooner drink rainwater from the gutters and the mullions,
Which tells you how much tea appeals to me.

In Boston many years ago
They had the right idea,
When tea was taxed, the rebels all said, 'No!'
They threw the tea in Boston bay and said, 'Get out of here.

And stick your tea-tax where the sun don't shine!'
This epithet's gone down in history,
But still it's drunk in gallons by countrymen of mine,
What they see in it is a mystery.

If you say you hate tea, people look at you all weird,
At least that is the way they look at me
And all because my system refuses to be geared
To the merits of a cup of bleedin' tea!

Mick Nash

THE PIPER OF AVIGNON

Into the heart of Avignon, the Palace Square,
Flute in his hand, a piper stepped and there
Smiled into his instrument and began to play,
Thaïs, Méditation, by Jules Massenet,
Sweet notes, evocative, beguiling, pure and clear,
Rose to the Papal Palace, tall and stern, severe,
And through each window, up and down each stair,
Cadences flowed like liquid, silken air,
Round lofted pillar, underneath steep arch, compressed,
Shimmered and in high-vaulted ceiling came to rest.
I was seduced, enchanted, held in thrall
By music bitter-sweet and mystical,
Had he been Hamelin's piper, I a city son,
I would have followed him forever and perchance have won
The vision most celestial, but alas,
Like Hamelin's cripple boy left outside on the grass,
When I emerged, piper and flute were gone,
I was alone, bereft, in Avignon.

Barry Jones

'Jecano' Unexpected

Something ready; waiting there
Arriving audience is part aware
With preparing trio, into sound
The energetic group at gentle stage
Musicians ready to engage.

Round faces seen; illuming beam
Only three make up the team
Positioned firmly on their ground,
Drums upstage take central place
Spaced guitars triangle trace.

Moderate start is sparked alive,
The instruments to overdrive,
Power dragon voice around
Gruff and musically intense,
Echoes through excited audience.

Vocal Arthur; also lead guitar,
John on bass, no lesser star,
With so much action to be found,
So count the drumsticks if you can
Worked by demon drummer Dan.

Fast notes and not a single tangle,
Projecting out from the triangle,
Creating music in the mound,
Potential to a new volcano
Is powerful pyramid, 'Jecano.'

Reg C H Baggs

THE TREES OF CHRISTMAS

Around the byways of my life entwined,
The trees of Christmas in my memory grow;
Paths leading to eternity I find.

The fir trees' resin-scents awake my mind
To childhood's wonder, lit by candle-glow,
Around the byways of my life entwined.

Blood-berried holly as a festive wreath I bind;
Symbol of thorns which crowned my Saviour's brow;
Paths leading to eternity I find.

The kisses of a lifetime, true and kind,
Strung pearls of love, white-berried mistletoe;
Around the byways of my life entwined.

Incense from myrrh and frankincense refined,
Sweet breath from Heaven perfumes earth below;
Paths leading to eternity I find.

Evergreen memories woven in my mind,
Patterns of pleasures past, before me flow;
Around the byways of my life entwined
Paths leading to eternity I find.

Eileen Burgess

WHO'S A PRETTY GIRL THEN?

You can still be nifty
At fifty,
Don't bother about fifty,
Assert
Yourself in a new
Micro-skirt,
Don't worry about fifty,
Just flirt!

Geoff Fenwick

For You

I'm the one for you
But you can't see
I'm feeling blue
Come rescue me

I'm giving up friends
To spend time with you
But that's a waste of time
If I can't be close to you

I'm afraid I may have to let go
Before I get too close
You're a drug which could probably
Cause an overdose

I want to let it out
And tell you how I'm feeling
But I'm afraid you'll break the heart
That is only just healing

Don't play me around
I can't afford to get hurt
Do you have feelings
Or are you just a flirt?

The only thing that can stop us
From being apart
Is for you to tell me
I'm in your heart

So I'm singing this song
To tell you I won't do you wrong
And together we belong
Or am I the one who is so wrong?

Simon McAlear

OUR HOUSE

Georgian? Yes, George the fifth - small rooms.
Period? Well, yes, post World War I.
Built in one of thirties' building booms.
Pedigree? Its history's just begun.
Here once cattle grazed and grasses grew
Beneath a roof of sky. Lamps were stars.
Wife remembers cattle driven through
Where broken kerbs house ungaraged cars.

Semi-detached, end of block, two floors;
Bath, WC (or loo) combined;
Two beds, box, with painted, panelled doors;
Two rooms, kitchen down, with lawn behind.
Tongue of time has licked the fields away;
Farm folded up, let our road come through;
Hands piled bricks instead of making hay.
Wife recalls when sheep came into view.

No chairs of Chippendale: just a set
In oak, matching sideboard, handed down.
Which of our relations, I forget.
Three-piece suite in tapestry, in brown.
No Morris walls or Robert Adam work;
No television star, household name.
Inside no one ever went berserk,
Leaving us the burden of his shame.

Neighbours leave their prints on memories,
Foreign faces climb the garden wall,
Admiration for our apple trees,
Offspring make acquaintance with a ball.
Will, in future years, our house conform?
Or identity just disappear?
Or will spirit of the place inform
Passer-by, a versifier once lived here?

F G Ward

Why?

I walked into town today
And I walked White Wickets' way,
Over the field where the daisies stipple
Their dew-washed petals on fresh green lea;
With buttercups in bloom, gilded bright,
It truly was a beautiful sight
Painted, I know, for you and for me.

I strolled by the football pitch
Close to the hedge where some wretch,
With no thought for those who walk for pleasure,
Had left squashed beer cans and plastic bags;
He had carried them when full, so why
Leave them when empty under the sky
Among a litter of stubbed-out fags?

N M Beddoes

The Surprise Gift

Eric went a-cockling one bright and sunny day,
He thought, *I know a lady who would like a taste of they.*
So home he trots with buckets full and says to Vi, his wife,
'Now get these cooked and put in jars and seasoned up with spice.'
So Vi got busy with the pans and cooked, they looked a treat,
Eric said, 'You've done that well - they look good enough to eat.'
He picks them up and off he goes across his garden gay,
Knocks at No17 saying, 'What time are you away?
I've got a little offering here I want to send with you,
They're really meant for Topsy, but I'm sure you'll get a few.
I'd really like to see her face when you stand them on her table,
But as I am so far away of course I'll be unable.
Now let me know just what she says when these cockles she espies,
Just tell the truth and don't come back with a pack of lies.'
Now Barbara's back and Eric thinks the truth will now unfold,
Did Topsy like the cockles, or did they leave her cold
Topsy saw the cockles, said, 'Oh what a treat.'
A nicer gent than Eric you'd never, ever meet.
The moral of this story is very plain to see,
If you want to please a lady, send some cockles for her tea.

Barbara King

A Pause For Thought

Oh Lord,
You made our earth and sky,
The beasts and humble butterfly.
Your glory's there for all to see,
That majesty, I hear, is thee.

Why did you make the moon and stars?
Obnoxious folk, who drive fast cars
And fishes in the deep blue sea,
Why go to all that pain for me?

You made the earth quite fast they say
And rested on the Sabbath day.
Mistakes you made are clear to see,
Like horrid germs, and maybe me.

Your commandments; as I live and sleep
Are things I find so hard to keep.
And sin; you tempt me day and night,
I often ask, *can this be right?*

I haven't been to church to pray
On this, or any other day.
I guess you know, all things you see,
Why don't you show yourself to me?

We live, we breathe and when we die
We end up somewhere in the sky.
All very strange, you must agree.
So . . . What's in it for you and me?

Richard Lee Nettleton

WHY?

Why are summer skies so blue
And green corn turn to gold?
Why does the north wind have to blow
And turn the autumn cold?

Why do I love the summer rain
That falls so soft and warm?
Why do I fear the lightning flash
Through a wild electric storm?

Why do the seasons come and go,
Or day turn into night?
Why does the moon, so high above,
Shine with her silvery light?

Why is my heart still beating
When I feel like I have died?
Why do I fear the lonely nights
Without him by my side?

Why must the golden autumn leaves
Fall almost overnight?
Why does the snowy landscape melt
As soon as all is white?

Why do others break our hearts
And leave us sad and low?
Why does the sea rush to the shore
While rivers gently flow?

Why do I fear the shadows so,
When all alone at night?
Why do the birds start singing
As soon as it is light?

When my life has reached the end
And it's time for me to go,
The answer to these questions
I'm sure I'll never know.

Marisa Greenaway

THE OLD OAK TREE

The old man lay 'neath the old oak tree,
Lay with his friend, his dog, and me.
As the sun scorched down from way up high,
It sizzled the grass, now brown and dry.
He reached for his lute and played it low,
The music around us seemed to flow.
The dog scampered round and jumped for joy,
Then chased a leaf, as though a toy.
Combined with the scent of new-mown hay,
'Twas a perfect, blissful, summer day.

But as the winter closes in,
And the winds blow cold, and the air gets thin,
The old man visits the tree much less,
And stays by the fire, with his old dog, Bess.
Till summer, he'll stay where it is drier,
Till the weather's warm and the sun gets higher.
Then again he will go to the old oak tree,
With his old dog Bess, his friend and me.

Richard & Kathleen Hill

My Cat Billy Boy

Give me a beautiful cat who likes to doze,
To spare the time of living,
Somebody who talks with me and knows
Of both loving and forgiving.

A true friend who can accept my sighs
And tally my virtues so clear,
To remain faithful at the end of the day,
What then I have to fear
As my cat is always so near?

Sammy Michael Davis

Rhymes

I like my poems to rhyme,
Whatever modern people say,
I just go on in my own sweet way,
I'm not caught up in their sway.
I'd sooner rhyme it any day.
I like my poems to rhyme.

When I get pressure from high places,
I just keep kicking at my traces.
I could laugh right in their faces
And match them all in any paces,
I like my poems to rhyme.

They say my rhyming is archaic,
I could make my verses more prosaic.
To make them more intellectual,
Would render them ineffectual.
I like my poems to rhyme.

June Worsell

THE WRITING CLASS

Writing course 'tis today
we've all come out to play
tutor *will* have her say
how her voice thundered!

I haven't got a care
my mind completely bare
I simply sit and stare
my days are numbered.

Miss says, 'You'll never pass!
You're just a silly ass
you're bottom of the class
out of one hundred.'

Quills to the left of me
quills to the right of me
quills all encircle me
my work they've plundered.

I'm simply so afraid
at home I wish I'd stayed
what a mistake I made
oh how I blundered.

What if I'd never come?
Was ever one so dumb?
'Please Miss, I want my mum!'
'Bad luck, you're lumbered!'

George E Jones

IN A WORD

Words to witter and to eat
Worthy diet, Babel meat,
Seeming wholesome, sounding naff,
Part exchanged in wordy gaff,
Thrown away to ride the air
Bull's-eye honed with awesome care,
Woolly nonsense, weighty fare,
Talking peace, indulging war,
Scoring points upon the jaw,
Lifting up and putting down
Legacy of king and clown,
Carved on stone, recording time,
Telling stories, ringing rhyme,
Everlasting, ever new,
Words subscribe the me to you.

Shirley Johnson

STILL FAITHFUL

The old man he put down his paper
And moved the grey cat from his knee
He reached for his stick, although not very quick
And he rose from the comfort and ease.

The dog watched his master intently
Got up from the mat where he lay,
He knew the routine, each day they had been
To his mistress at her time of day.

With his coat and his hat he was ready
And took a last look at the room.
The cat he would wait, but the dog at the gate
Made it clear he would not go alone.

They went down the lane so familiar,
The path that they always loved best
And they turned at the bend, the old man and his friend
To visit his wife - now at rest.

Dorothy Blakeman

The Good Partner

When the weather's bright and fine,
The sun shines in the sky,
Our spirits are uplifted,
We have no wish to cry.
But when the sky grows darker
And rain falls from above,
It's when we are unhappy
That we need someone to love.
Someone who will listen
When life's plans have gone astray,
Someone to rejoice with you
When things have gone your way,
To help to share your burdens
And also ease the pain,
A love to keep you going
Until the sun returns again.

M L Oliver

IT'S ON THE TIP OF MY TONGUE

What *is* that word I want to use?
I think it starts with 'ren',
It isn't 'rental', that's not it.
I nearly had it then!

He worked for an insurance firm,
That tall chap with a bike.
What was his name? He knew that girl
That had a brother, Mike.

We went by bus. You know the place.
We had a lovely meal.
No, not that one, the other one,
It sounds a bit like Deal.

'You know the song I mean,' I say,
The tune goes la-de-dum.
What were the words? The middle verse
Begins with, "He's a bum."'

What was she called? That girl in class.
The blonde girl. Was it Lynnet?
Don't think about it, let it drop,
You'll get it in a minute!

Anne Gardiner

The Traveller

One night I camped in a field of grain
all it did was rain and rain.
When I awoke I was soaking wet,
upon leaving the field almost collided with the vet.
Travelling on for hours and hours
at dusk I camped in a field of flowers.
Next morning when I awoke
on the perfume I did choke.
So I went again on my way
till the fading light of day.
Where I came across a field of muddy brown,
pitched my tent and then settled down.
I ended up camping on slimy clay.
When travelling and camping
this is normally the way.
Constantly moving on every day
is not much fun I have to say.

S Glover

NIGHT OF THE BIG WIND

The wind swept off the mountains,
Came howling down the glen,
The trees they roared in protest
And swayed like drunken men.

Grass rippled like a river,
Bracken swirled like ocean foam,
Leaves rattled on the window,
The chimney raised a moan.

A crash outside informed us
The old spruce had met its doom,
Soot fell on the hearthstone,
Smoke billowed round the room.

We huddled around the fireside
And listened to the din,
'We won't go short of firewood,'
Said Granny, with a grin!

Terry O'Reilly

A Lovely Song To God

Let's all sing a lovely song
That's not too short and not too long,
That thanks and praises God our king,
Who listens to the words we sing.

This is how our song will go,
A song we'll all soon come to know.
That's not too short and not too long,
So let's all sing this lovely song.

We thank you Lord for everything,
For voices so that we can sing
Our thanks and praises Lord to you,
For everything for us you do.

We thank you Lord that you're our king,
That we can all rejoice and sing.
You are the truth, the life, the way,
For this we'll praise you Lord each day.

We thank you Lord, you'll hear our song
That's not too short and not too long.
Accept our thanks and praises too,
Lord in this song we sing to you.

Royston Davies

THE PRISONER

Prisoner here in one's own mind,
The dept not yet repaid in kind.
Face up to the facts that sound the day,
The captor's aims are for you to stay.
Escape the torture, the great assault,
Change your ways and correct your faults,
Social outcast, no one more,
Even the thief, the liar and whore.
Bitter feelings are all that remain,
Hatred and anger difficult to restrain.
Chasing thoughts of being free,
One day it may all well be.

Jondaniel Harris

A Walk With Nature

We strolled by Dockens Water,
One early day in spring,
Daffodils fluttering in the woods,
Wild geese upon the wing.

We saw some natural habitats,
Some footprints in the sand,
We saw the wild fowl on the lake,
Binoculars in our hand.

A coppice of weeping willow,
Near where the roe deer run,
A lesson in nature study,
A dipping pond, what fun!

A garden with a water butt
To catch the falling rain,
Plants to attract the butterflies
When the sun shines again.

The mallards gliding by quite near,
The grebe play side by side,
A cormorant and a goldeneye,
Unaware we are in a 'hide.'

A kingfisher in the trees above,
But soon it flies away,
The buzzards flapping way up high,
It was such a splendid day.

June Melbourn

BRIEF REVELATION

In winter, murky mists each morning fall
And shroud the marsh in doleful mystery,
Whilst in the dykes the moorhen's muffled call
Is all that mars the tranquil symmetry;
And on the point the lighthouse blinks to sea,
An answer to the foghorn's repartee.

Yet as the day draws on to afternoon,
The sun's wan rays break through the wafting mist.
The marsh is seen unveiled, but all too soon
Is lost, as if it never did exist;
And once again the mist lies over all,
Again the distant foghorns start to call.

Jax Burgess

THE OLD MAN

Picture the old man down the street,
With his back so bent and so slow of feet.
His face all worn and so sad at his plight,
Oh how he wished he could be all right.
Imagine that same man when he was young,
With his eyes so bright and full of fun.
Think of the things he may have done,
The places he had been, the conquests fought and won.
Once he laughed and joked as you like to do,
So try to remember, someday this could be you.

Shirley Wasylyk

IT'S EARLY DAYS YET

They were married in the early spring
It seemed to be the proper thing
Some pessimists took on a bet -
But then, it's early days as yet.

She looked fantastic in a dress
Fit for the prettiest princess
Swathed in finest floating net -
But then, it's early days as yet.

They had a honeymoon in Spain
Marred by quite unseasonal rain
They drank too much, got into debt -
But then, it's early days as yet.

An only child, she craved a baby
He wanted time and just said, 'Maybe'
The waiting sadly made her fret -
But then, it's early days as yet.

She did night work and met a lover
They consummated undercover
Had pessimists thus won their bet?
But then, it's early days as yet.

She grew in confidence - and size
Pregnant to experienced eyes
They called the baby Simon Bret -
But still, it's early days as yet.

Her husband said, 'It *could* be mine,'
Maybe they'll do that test in time
For DNA - or just forget
But then, it's early days as yet.

V Jean Tyler

A September Sunset

The golden glow of a September sunset
casts shadows across the verdant grass.
The dying sun and the onset of evening
remind me again that all things must pass.
A crow is cawing from a nearby rooftop
and midges are dancing in the twilight air.
Tonight the garden is fresh and vibrant
but tomorrow I will see fallen leaves there.
We have but a brief time to work and play;
we must be bold and seize the day.

Andrew Banks

EMMA'S SNOW POEM

Snow falling in the night,
Moonlight shining bright,
Sparkling crystals light
Glisten in the starry height.
Feathers fly from the sky,
Drop down to earth and die.
Turning into diamond shine,
Riches from another time.

Sun rises, sky blue,
Now the day is very new.
Children jump out of beds,
Putting hats upon their heads,
Cosy coats to keep them warm.
Running out at crack of dawn,
Building snowmen on the lawn.

Sledges slide down the hill,
Shouting, skidding, never still.
Tumbling over heaps of snow,
Overhead the snowballs go.
Sliding on the slippery ice,
Falling over once or twice.

Next day comes the rain,
Snow melts away again.
Falls from houses with a thud,
Leaves behind the slush and mud.

Jessica Ruggles, Ruth, Beth & James Allan

TROLLEY FOLLY

Please 'superstores', modernise trolleys,
At present they're hard to control.
It's easy for those young and healthy,
But we oldies are sent up the pole!

Trolleys wait till they're full with our goodies,
Then develop a mind of their own.
Go straight? You *are* joking - not likely,
We'll go every which way so you'll moan!

We reach home completely exhausted,
With aches and pains taking their toll.
We haven't the strength to push trolleys
Insisting on doing rock and roll!

So please, if you still want our custom,
Design trolleys all smooth and sublime,
Then we'll shop in your stores with much pleasure,
Instead of dreading our visit each time . . .

Paddy Jupp

A Dream Of Tranquillity

Walking dreamily through the forest, 'twas approaching twilight,
Drinking in the scent of fragrant flowers on a warm summer's night.
The sultry air feeling humid I glance up, bewitched by the spell
of the moon.
Daylight slips away, but the atmosphere remains harmonious, by
nature's noisome tune.

I continue to walk on inquisitively, enchanted by the forest's charm.
I feel a sense of security here, far away from any harm.
The breeze begins to pick up now, I shudder with the chill,
The restless trees sway listlessly, ceasing to remain so still.

I press on and yonder, gasp, what a sight!
I screw up my eyes and look ahead of me into the night.
The forest had truly come alive and as far as my eyes could see,
Were countless different animals, who'd come out to welcome me.

I start to feel fatigued and lie down beneath the bough of an old
oak tree.
I gaze up into the heavens, where I know God is watching me.
I gasp in awe at the countless stars and vastness of the sky,
My heart leaps with joy and overwhelmed, I begin to cry.

I feel as though I have stood right at the top of the world tonight
And looked down on creation, filling my soul with delight.
I suddenly awake abruptly . . . I sit up, rigid in my bed,
I now begin to realise it's all a dream, a mere fantasy in my head.

Emma Thackway

PARTING COMPANY

The partnership is over, what has gone wrong?
Where once there was harmony, there's a worn out song.

Where once there was love, there are vindictive jibes.
Long gone is the tenderness and the passionate vibes.

They've tried years for a solution, still it's all gone bad,
The teenage children don't live with both their mum and dad.

What of the future, after all the pain?
Two middle-aged people will be starting again.

Maybe a new partner, perhaps even a new name,
Which one of the dysfunctional couple deserves all the blame?

Both in their fifties, a strange time to roam,
Just another statistic, too close to home.

Trevor Napper

BIRD SONG

The clamorous dawn chorus awakes the sleeping night
As countless happy songsters acclaim the new daylight.
Slowly the golden circle ascends the eastern sky
And the shimmering hot air rises on a somnalent midday.
Soaring in the Heaven, the lark throbs his ecstatic tune
The song of noon.

The setting sun's bright circle dips beyond the world's rim
While in the darkening dome of sky the glowing colours dim.
As evening's purple shadows spread an ever growing pall
The magic hush of twilight holds all creatures in its thrall
And in a million gardens a blackbird claims his vantage point
To herald night.

Soon the etherial moon will work her magic transformation
Painting the world in mystery as she seeks her destination
How eerie familiar objects seem in her unaccustomed ray
As etched in black and silver, through the spangled velvet sky
Comes the mournful tawny owl, the embodied spirit of the night,
In silent flight.

Olive Cragg

My Part

It shouldn't have taken long to learn
But I never quite perfected the part.
A few throw away lines
Then off stage left.

Do we shout and scream
Throw our hands up in despair
Or look long and meaningful
At some empty chair?

So many banal pages scanned
In the search for a perfect blend.
Dreams and reality side by side,
Pointless words and movement without end.

I meet the other bemused players
Pretend my conversation is real.
Tho' it's only a part I play
I'm sure any rester would steal.

Somewhere beneath it all
Maybe a character of depth.
For now I swim in shallow water
And milk the applause to death.

John Marshall

AVEBURY'S ANCIENT STONES

A place of magic and mystery,
Ritual and ceremonial history -

The henge of Avebury's circle of stone
Is the largest one that Britain has known:

Enclosed by a roughly circular bank
With a flat-bottomed ditch on the inner flank;

And area of twenty-eight acres of land
Where over a hundred sarsen stones stand;

Twice seven by seven encircled the dip,
Just seven metres inside the lip;

An inner circle of twenty-nine,
With twelve small stones in a crooked line;

And the obelisk, a monolith,
Posing another question in the henge's myth;

And to the north are two other rings
Encircling The Cove at the centre of things;

What it all meant is still unknown -
That's the magic of Avebury's circle of stone.

Joy Morton

THE RHYMESTER

Here's to a poem with a rhyme
Supporting rhythm and a beat,
In measured stanzas and a time
Which prompts a tapping of the feet.

Recorded in iambic form
Consistent with a four foot norm,
To discipline the lip and tongue,
Clear, like a peal of bells well rung.

Perhaps to tell how song-birds sing
As dawn and dusk they herald in,
Or mimicking the turtle-dove
With passion fired to speak of love.

Some may excite or animate
While others aim to speculate,
Divergent or in uniform,
Ad hoc or planned all may perform

To amplify their chosen patch -
The window nestling in the sash?
The door engaging with the latch?
Or e'en the hand which holds a catch?

Or patterns from Creation's scene
Arranged by chromosome and gene,
'Mid healing of the summer's breeze
And cleansing of the winter's freeze.

In normal times with all that said,
There's welcome in the poet's bed
For diverse ones to rest awhile,
Adversely pondering their style -

But for this once to be quite frank
We wish them not to write in 'Blank'.

Gordon Padgett

HALL PORTER

I sits the while, sees it all
pass me by along the 'all;
raw or sad, it's in me gaze -
life's the same beneath the glaze.

No 4, well, she's a case,
'ad four babies in disgrace;
now 'er plays the game at 'ome -
got too old to go an' roam.

'Im's so smart at No 10,
often fancies other men;
gay's the times they 'ave up there -
poncy clothes an' perfumed 'air.

6 is old an' never moves,
stuck in 'is old, fuddy groves;
milk piles up outside 'is door -
'ee don't know what birds are for!

The 'andsome one is No 8,
comes on telly very late;
nightly 'as a different bird,
now 'ee's on 'is forty-third.

3's the bloke I always mind -
real gent 'ee is, all posh and kind;
if I knows the where an' when
's worth the odd quid now and then.

'Ere - you the new one to arrive?
Just come empty, No 5;
'is 'earse looked fine all polished black -
served 'im right for 'itting back.

Edward Fursdon

GOOD NEWS

There's a rainbow in the sky
For God's promise will not die
And the Word that He has spoken stands for aye
When we see that splendid arc
In a sky that's dull and dark
It uplifts our drooping spirits right away.

Oh, our sky is often dark
On our lives it leaves its mark
It should bring us to our knees before His throne
There is safety in this place
There the storms of life abate
But we try to bear our burdens all alone.

We are from the earth the dust
That which was created first
But the Hand that made and formed us is divine
And the spirit which he gave
With such power and such care
Made of us a living being for all time.

There's good news for everyone
In our place there stood a man
From the Glory He came down to pay the debt
He had opened up a way
When death's darkness on Him lay
And the Father's just requirements He had met.

See the rainbow in the sky
Know God's promise will not die
For who-so-ever comes the price is paid
And there's still an empty place
And it's still the day of grace
And the angels will rejoice when you are saved.

Catherine Macdonald

TIGER IN THE WILDERNESS

She was my first belovéd cat,
    When I was six, no more.
She wore three rings about her neck
    And bracelets on each paw.
Her tiger stripes were black and clear,
    Her coat was fawn and grey,
And green and shining were her eyes,
    Inviting me to play.
A handsome clump of ribbon-grass
    Grew near the kitchen door,
A newly planted garden ours
    Where none had been before.
The earth was clay, the top-soil stripped
    Before they built our house,
And hard my father worked to grow
    Mere shelter for a mouse.
The ribbon-grass, a graceful plant,
    Became his modest pride,
When fully grown in summertime
    A kitten there could hide.
So *Kitty* found it her delight
    She pounced, she beat it down.
My kindly father let her play
    Without reproof or frown.
And when within its patterned shade
    She laid her weary head,
'A tiger in the wilderness,'
    Was what my father said.

Kathleen M Hatton

OUT OF SEASON

Storm darkened waves roll in high,
Clean the sand with whitest foam,
Lately rain-washed pale blue sky
With watery sun the droplets comb.
Gulls tossed in frivolous breeze,
Formed, re-formed at its whim,
Moving, swooping, chalk white frieze
Yacht-like using wings to trim.
The coastline shrouded in a haze
A wind-blown curtain made of spray,
Grains of sand exposed flesh graze,
Scarves and hoods blown away.
Beach caught in the groyne's lea,
Safeguarding castles for next year,
Treasures cast up by the sea,
Spring tides sweeping hollows clear.
No one lingers on the shore
Save fishermen who search the scour,
What difference in a few months more
Tourists will crowd each sunlit hour.

Di Bagshawe

MOTION

Anything that comes to mind
    Take your time
        Moves in motion
            Motion in time

Open space, clear blue sky
    Moving traffic
        Blue eyes
            Melting rain
                Billboards in grime.

Terry Lane

BROKEN

She stands all alone, expressionless stare,
Lost part of her soul, but she doesn't know where.

Blood runs down her cheek, and drips from her chin,
She looks at her body, so tired and thin.

She thought that she loved him, but his temper exploded,
Now love's broken down, decayed and corroded.

Days and weeks fade away, months and years lost in fear,
She cries every night, but the neighbours don't hear.

Her hands won't stop shaking as she lights a cigarette,
She aches for a feeling that's not pain, or regret.

Her head is a mess of anger and commotion,
When did she last have a positive emotion?

Her reflection looks back, tears still in her eyes,
His key turns in the door . . . another part of her dies.

Neil Brown

WHAT LIES AHEAD

The trouble with life moments ahead,
Unexpected happens people have said.
Perhaps it is good, for us not to know
Live our lives daily, till we have to go.

We plan for a future, which is unknown
When bad does occur, we are not alone.
This great someone living somewhere
Knows of our problems really does care.

I've been there I know this invisible God
When I'm at my worst, he's keeping a log.
He sends someone to me to help me along
What I think impossible to him it's a song.

He smoothes out the pathway lying ahead
Gently he rocks me, like a baby in bed
I feel his great comfort, in what has to be
I truthfully know he will never leave me.

Joan Prentice

WORDS

Words can be listened to through the ear,
Out of the mouth they appear.
Invisible, out of reach,
Known as speech.
Part of existence since the spelling of dot,
Long may words be spoken a lot.
Remember nice words are kind,
Some should be left behind.

Janet Degnan

THE YORKSHIRE ROSE

Just a good old English rose tree carried home with tender care,
    A special breed, a pure white Yorkshire rose so very rare;
My promise to present to you which I hopefully did pray
    Would enchant the dour old Scottish Thistle o'er the border way.

Dormant within its petals lies a dream you could not know,
    Enchanting wild elusive deep and white as drifting snow;
Should my verse unto a stranger bear a sentimental ring
    Is it really so surprising that I once proclaimed you King?

Since you left this English rose tree without another thought
    In a stranger's Scottish garden and valued it as nought,
May it ever bloom abundant, each petal kissed by morning dew,
    For that special English rose is oh so Yorkshire through
                                      and through.

Margaret Marsh

THE GYPSY

Every year he stayed a while,
Sun-tanned face and beaming smile.
'RIP' his dog was round and fat,
An ancient tabby, he just called 'Cat'.

This tall and handsome gypsy man
With his brightly painted horse drawn van,
He would sharpen knives, mend wicker chairs
Then late at night would set his snares.

He sold heather, pegs and hand carved dolls,
Pills and potions for troubled souls.
Trim the hedges, clean the ditch
Make baskets from the willow switch.

He told stories of the days of old,
The autumn leaves of red and gold.
Tales of wise, old gypsy kings
Of badgers, foxes, of many things.

Sometimes he played his violin,
Then we children would dance and sing.
And when the autumn evenings glow,
Like swifts and swallows he would go.

Every year he stayed a while,
Sun-tanned face and beaming smile.
'RIP' his dog was round and fat,
An ancient tabby, he just called 'Cat'.

K S Nunn

RHYME AND REASON

Poetry I feel comes from within
Rhyming word, that makes the heart sing
The mind and heart, right from the soul
Unrhyming poetry, I feel is droll
When poetry rhymes, it pleases the eye
Don't others try, I ask myself why
I've always thought poetry's a gift
To tell a story, give another a lift
Send someone you love, a word from the heart
Tell of your love whenever apart
Or all of the beauty all over the land
Poetic words of kindness, so all understand
Each word will come, from inside with love
Heart, mind and soul and Heaven above
Call on your feelings, and you'll surely find
Poetry like love, should never be blind
This you will find, time after time
The written word of poetry, should always rhyme.

C S Fricker

DANCING WITH THE DEVIL!

He walked my way a rare jewel,
I loved him he smiled so beautiful.
But he played with me the game of fool.

I trusted him, my pal, my friend,
I thought we could reach the rainbow's end.
But that was not to be,
As he secretly poured his evil over me.

I was in the wispy clouds of love,
Too late I would have known,
If God hadn't stepped in,
And then the truth was shown.

God took me on a journey,
We travelled very deep.
He took me to the devil's home,
Where captured souls, Satan would keep.

There within the imprisoned crowd,
The smug devil showed his face.
I saw it was my pal, my friend,
Living in an evil place.

He was dancing on the dark side,
Where there was no sun.
Dallying with the devil,
They became as one.

The satanic dream to murder,
Drawing blood is in their head!
The devil gave him so much strength,
He secretly stabbed me with all he said.

But God is a guide on the pathway of life,
And God teaches us to climb over the stiles.
A lesson, don't judge by appearances,
For the truth is hidden within the mind's files.

He walked my way a rare jewel,
I loved him he smiled so beautiful.

Carol Ann Darling

Hostilities

The effects of war are dire to behold.
Innocent children suffer, animals die,
and the real stories will never be told.

The rulers of our world are full of greed,
they don't care about orphans or waifs,
nor if men and women starve and bleed.

They want the other people's lands,
all the hills, dales, trees and flowers,
all the islands, oceans and desert sands.

For land puts money in their purse,
then fame and glory follow on,
but the loser's life is made much worse.

Would that I could change this earth,
put everything back to rights
and see that each man has his worth.

But while human beings are around
there is no chance of that.
Nor will peace and happiness ever be found.

Daf Richards

WHIFF WITH JOY

The phone did ring; heart skipped a beat,
Terena calling? Chance to meet?
The answer yes, TB, that cutie
Suggested we go to the 'Sleeping Beauty'!
Joy I felt and with great care,
I washed my body and my hair,
So when Terena came, the smell
Would be from Heaven, not from Hell!
We went, we parked, the tickets got
And found our seats - a row C slot.
We saw the man, but didn't think
He'd spread bad odours, skunk like stink!
The ballet started, most exquisite,
Just the job for our second visit.
Beautiful colours, those pas de deux,
Those graceful movements - quel bon heur!
But then our nostrils went skew-whiff,
We couldn't believe it, and wondered if
A toilet door was open, ajar,
Blowing bad vapours to cause this faux pas!
At the interval we drank Earl Grey,
Terena said, 'Let's move away.'
And so we did; it got a bit better,
Manageable but still like feta.
Back to the ballet, a wondrous show,
A credit indeed to 'The Ballet Moscow'.
But we'll always remember, it will always cloy
That we had to endure that whiff with joy!

John Birkett

Voyage Of Dreams

I dreamt I was sailing to Minever, on a boat with a billowed sail
There was no call for alarm; the sea was quite calm
With a mist like a virgin's veil
The captain was a fearless man, revered by his crew
They would serve him well; they would go through hell
For each man had his job to do
The skies were growing darker when the wind picked up the deep
It started to howl and the old sea dogs growled
As Neptune awoke from his sleep.

No one would rest on this dreadful night
Everyone knew they were in for a fight
Neptune would not be giving a quarter
He was master of all the oceans of water
The boat tossed and turned, some sails were lost
But no man left his station whatever the cost.

I saw the white of lightning, I heard the voice of thunder
The gods of the deep cried out in their sleep
That a good ship was going under
Neptune roared from beneath and gnashed his teeth
He could calm the troubled sea
The moon gave light to an awesome sight
That will stay forever with me
We buried the dead in the morning, wrapped in a white cotton veil
Tears fell like rain; I will not sail again
On a boat with a billowed sail.

Diane Howard

SAMANTHA (ONE-YEAR-OLD)

As she wanders around the house
Swiftly, like a tiny little mouse
Her face is creased in a wide smile
Not once or twice, but all the while
Now for everyone who meets her
She will give them all a fair share
Samm chatters to them one and all
But to some she gives a loud call
With the dog she just loves to play
Not that he has so much to say
It's only when she is asleep
Does he pretend to earn his keep
By barking at all who should come
To wake her up and start the fun
Sleeping sound she is loved by all
And her charm causes all to fall
Under the spell she is weaving
We show sorrow at her leaving
When the bright sun as ceased to shone
Sleepy, to her bed she has gone
Knowing she's settled to her slumber
We seem depleted in number
Perhaps to you it may seem queer
Samm to us is so very dear
Today her story we unfold
And she is only one-year-old.

Len Beddow

All That Glitters...

The past's shattered image
in a glass held hostage
to blur its fractures
shrouding its failures.

The crazed image remains,
with insolent indifference,
to re-enforce the strains
of a betrayed innocence.

The captive memory
held in moral obligation,
forgetting past fallibility,
in present stark reflection.

The cracked image kept
intact by corporate gloss:
hiding every venal fact
that profits bear a loss.

Michael Alan Fenton

RURAL AND DOMESTIC BYGONES

    Reminders of days gone-by,
now well beneath these waters lie.
The fields and farms, church, chapel, school,
all rest below the water cool.

    Rescued items link us still,
to what once was, and always will.
Reminders of both work and play,
pleasures and toils of yesterday.

    No longer used, but treasured,
momentoes of past times measured
now by memories, and tales told
around the fire when nights are cold.

Jo Brookes

BRIAN'S APPENDICITIS

I heard you'd gone to hospital
So I thought I'd write a verse
To say I hoped you'd soon be well
Instead you just got worse

Onto the operating table
They put you - around five
Which left us all wondering
Would you remain alive?

But alas the doctor knew his job
And with knife and scalpel clean
He cut out your appendix
And sewed a nice neat seam

It's obvious you've been a trial
To the nurses who cared for you
For two days later you were home
They threw you out - about two

I suppose you now must take a rest
And football cannot play
Or even walk to the local pub
For your pints of beer each day

I've had a word with the landlord
And a solution we have found
With several yards of hosepipe
We'll tap it underground

So if you now are wondering
Why suddenly friends appear
It's because they heard the rumour
That you've got a supply of beer!

Sandra Kinnear

HE'S HERE

He's here in your darkness,
Sending you a beam of light.
He's here in your blindness,
Only He can give you sight.

He's here no matter what
Others may think of you.
He's here no matter what
Others may do to you.

He's here, He'll show you the way,
Comfort you every day.
He's here, you're never alone,
Safe in His arms, He'll bring you home.

Natalie Jagger

The Ancient Horseman

The ancient horseman mounts his steed
    and looks upon the land,
So starts his journey to the east
    from dunes of burning sand.
He knows the course his journey takes
    and faster he does ride,
To mount the hand of evening wind
    and take wing to the sky.

His cape unfurls upon his back
    and blankets all behind,
Contained within this twilight cloak
    the evening stars do shine,
That spread to the horizon
    as his cadence gathers speed,
He crouches low upon the back
    and clings to nimble steed.

The daytime sun can see this horseman
    riding in its wake,
Thus quickens pace toward safety
    of horizon he does make,
And takes with him the brightness
    of the never ending day,
Leaving all to stars and moon
    tucked in the horseman's cape.

Enshrouded now within this cloak,
    the earth give way to night,
Bathed in sleepy harbour
    of the twinkling starlight.
Yet high above and left unseen
    the horseman races on,
In his never ending journey
    just to catch the daytime sun.

J A Brown

FAREWELL TO KEPHALONIA

O land of everlasting sun thought I
Where shade was sparse and bright the sky
Where dripped the olive, swept in the sea
Deep greens her depths, so clear and free
Where Bougainvillaea sent forth her hue
Of glowing purple toned with blue
And morning glory lifted high
Her magic melody to the sky
Where bird in cage sang its sweet song
And cats appeared to join our throng
Where hill and vale and rock and lea
Flowed ever onward to the sea
But now there is in glorious land
Another sight than sea and sand
A searing flash in clouds on high
And vivid forks light up the sky
Torrents of rain unceasing pour
On this belovéd foreign shore
But so I shall return again
Come sun, come wind, come summer rain
And turn my face and breathe the air
In this dear land forever fair.

Pamela J Rolinson

Taking His Time

The fat man walks alone,
In a cloud of his own well being.
People cast votes and judge him,
All eyes open but not seeing.

Where he has been it doesn't matter,
He walks on by without a care.
Where he is going is not your business,
While the people stop and stare.

He's proud of the attention he is getting,
But his confidence doesn't show.
Thinking *I am monarch, I am king,*
And all those will bow and follow.

But then one little boy points out,
Says, 'Sir, I do not lie.
People are staring at your chicken suit,
And also at your open fly!'

Jamie Barnes

A Time For Rhyme

I love to hear the sound of the wind and rain
Blowing gently against my windowpane
Pitter-patter of his watery feet
As it gently lulls me to a deep, deep sleep.

Where I can dream of the bright, bright sun
Glistening through the golden trees
And when I can feast my eyes on turquoise seas
Where children happily play on golden sands
And lovers walk slowly, hand in hand.

This is why I love to hear
The wind and rain as it blows gently against my windowpane
Pitter-patter of its watery feet
As it gently lulls me to a deep, deep sleep.

Susan Stuart

SCENE (SEEN) FROM A HILLTOP

The bright sunlight dances
    on top of each crest
Of a lazy old river
        that snuggles its breast
In the nest of the land
    that lies warm in the sun;
A rich, patchwork quilt
    nature's carefully spun.

Soft, mellowly fields
        that brighten the land -
So skilfully blended; so
        carefully planned.
And scattered at will, pine
        trees hugging your gaze
Stretching up to the sun
        as they bask in its rays.

A quaint old thatched cottage
        sits sheltered below -
Tucked well in the hillside to
        cheat winds that blow.
Over your head call the birds
          as they fly
Mocking your presence so close to
          their sky.

The sun tiptoes out of the sky
        for his rest
And the valley sleeps on - snug and
          warm in its nest.

Hannah Yates

HEAVEN

Heather swaying to and fro
Way above, the sun's aglow
Sheep are feeding in the grass
The cars slow down as they pass
Down below, a rippling tide
Views aplenty far and wide
Foxgloves rustle in the breeze
Autumn comes with falling leaves
People walking hand in hand
Looking down on golden sand
Could I be at Heaven's door?
Not at all, this is Exmoor.

Peter Tilson

BABYLON STORIES
(Sermons on susceptibility)

Sir Cause-of-all Things-Just sits gleefully by the witness box,
defers to *Bettyre Knowlige*, and measures by the clock;
judges hard on facts that hardly make sense,
declares a hung jury and takes refuge on the fence . . .
his pretty faced scion wanders out such languid, high profile days,
fawning to loose worship and inflated with gushy praise
he trips nimbly down scurrilous alleys and sumptuous *public lavatories* . . .
thus the doey-eyed, glossy juvenile sits, and freely admits
that 20 such pre-pubescent horrors made up his *greatest hits!*
Songs for all seasons pilfered from out the past . . . and
so several million in royalties make such ditties last and last . . .
Hurried now, the fortuitous kind defer
to protect their illegitimate patch from thieves and petty plunder.
Obsessed with *just*, and *meticulous* to the *nth* degree
they pour out old wisdoms and pocket the exorbitant fee!
Matched for a tepid set, they scour the public purse,
rule for every motion to screw the common convert,
galled for such pleasure, the *wasted waif* portrays
a never-ending spiral of languid, solitary days.
F***ed forever! Now let this vacuous silence descend,
in solitary bedsits a thousand meagre lives pretend . . .
The fortunate debate the swings, and on their own fat neck convene
an amount so thoroughly outrageous, so obscene . . .
The herald of the fair end-time appears, flapping in dissent,
announces the current fashion of a 'well rounded parliament',
'there shall hot brains stand firm . . . against the so-called breach
to be spoilers of the shady deal and complex conceit.'
This smooth Dome, voted the future's glee, a pure celebration of self,
crammed to the lid with symbols of years of stolen wealth,
sits like a soapbox, on which the limp delegate admits
to 400,000 acres of 20th century bull****
'Behold!' The *Tired Announcer* whispers, in communion at the rail
where all her vacuous promises sit like some bastardised Holy Grail;

ledgers for a profit, to avoid the common levy,
whiles awhile in secret isles her prudent misogyny.
Chaos! Chaos! An anathema finely strained,
served on the backs of millions, heads bowed to the rising gale,
winds of steeped misery rise headlong to portray
the twisting sermon of an old queen's suitable birthday.
Vague, the mists of nostalgia's cataracted past,
where sermons declare the splendour of an Empire declined and lost;
the written word is largely cosmetic for the cruelty and rage
of an obsessive little island's so called *golden age*.
Who do they think they are trying to impress?
What is this life? If all we can is stare,
and tell ourselves, in truth we could really care . . .
The weasel smiles to profane the common noise,
and rallies the troops for another oil-fuelled enterprise!

Christopher Hayes

WINTER'S SONG

Pass the orchard I walked today
Un-trodden snow paved my way

The sky was heavy with snow afresh
Trees now naked . . . littered with old bird's nests

A squirrel jumped from branch to branch
Showing off his nimble dance.

The north wind twirled the untouched snow
Like ballerinas on tiptoe flow

On the pond ducks slip and slide
Hopeful for titbits from . . . whoever passes by

Not content with his icy scene
Winter whistles . . . like a banshee's scream!

Hands in pockets . . . I pushed them deep.
Jack Frost nipping and biting at hands and feet.

Pass the orchard . . . and past the pond
A welcome light in the distance shone.

A refuge safe . . . from winter's song.

Sylvia Connor

STREET POETRY

'Black, white and coloured cotton socks -
Three pairs for a pound.'

In the busy market place
The sweating vendor mops his face
And sings in robust English tongue
A trivial commercial song.

'Black, white and coloured cotton socks -
Three pairs for a pound.'

Could critic fault such economic choice
Of words pitched by his gravel voice,
Ignoring just how sweetly wound
This catchphrase of his rollsome round?

'Black, white and coloured cotton socks -
Three pairs for a pound.'

Terry Smith

HARMONY RE-ESTABLISHED

The harmonal tranquillity ripens beyond the devious grounds,
the restful nature considers departure, fretting sound.
Finding precious senses, undermining strength,
the silent ability deceives the phenomenal length.

Discovering acres of compulsive truth,
imbedding the findings in anonymous youth.
Judging the memorial recreations of renewable hope,
reversing the raw faith to unbeatable scope.

The enabling power infuriates the unknown,
that banishes oxygen, challenging the forces of peace alone.
Shattered by smithereens of eternal dirt,
whilst peace attempts replacing the forbidden sodden hurt.

The atmosphere delicately defines the pumping pulse,
exceptional strain makes the truth false.
Power so pure promised the naked flame,
whilst reluctant showers descend, fortified with golden rain.

Expedition of Mother Nature morally completed,
the renewable coincidental threat defeated.
Departure of deliberate hate banished,
love and peace excepted, hate and pain vanished.

Emma Davey

DRIVING

I cannot
See ahead,
The road
Beyond
Is
Dead
And beyond
And beyond.

Nicola Barnes

WRAITH

From the cradle to the grave
A masochistic slave
A dead man walking
Inner demons are always talking

Believe not in what you see
Choose how you define your reality
Hope that the only feeling isn't pain
What or who do you need to stay sane?
Who is your reason to remain?

Although there is darkness in my heart
I hope that in your life I can have a part
Spent too much time on my own
I cannot carry on alone.

Neil Parsons

THE WRESTLER

My breath became choked,
By his 'Half-Nelson' hold;
And the lights in the hall,
Turned to scarlet - from gold!

Must get free from his grip!
Came the thought to my mind
While the salt perspiration,
Was driving me blind!

I relaxed - for a moment,
Then I made a sharp grab;
Attempting to get on,
A swift 'Boston Crab'!

He was wise to my move,
It was easy to block;
For he dropped the 'Half-Nelson',
And employed a 'Head-Lock'!

But! - He hadn't foreseen,
That my move was a feint!
For I leapt off the canvas,
In manner so quaint!

He had lost his advantage,
My trick was quite rare!
From the ring he went sailing,
Done - by my 'Flying Mare'!

Ron Bissett

Enjoyment Of Poetry

Poetry is good and very calming,
I start to write it when I feel a bit alarming.
If things start to go very wrong,
I turn to poetry, maybe I could write a song.

It's easier to write down how I feel,
Because at times, some things seem so unreal.
So then I try to straighten things out,
It's nice to do it quietly without having to shout.

It's also a way of saying what's in your heart,
Especially when you and your loved ones are far apart.
It's even better when you enjoy your writing,
Once you start, you'll find it so inviting.

Take a quiet moment, a chill-out time,
Forget about the work, forget about the grime.
Put your pen to paper and have a little try,
Some things you write might even make you cry.

It's also a challenge you will find,
And at least you write what's on your mind.
So go for it, I'm sure you'll be okay,
Say what you feel, make someone's day.

Kathy Buckley

ALL OUT!

Tumbling, stumbling,
Joyfully bumbling
Five dogs run, skittering over the floor.
Crushing, rushing,
Jostling and pushing -
Five dogs squeeze desperately through the back door.
Barking, larking,
Energy-sparking -
Out in a jumble of fur, teeth and claw!

Rosemary Williams

The Last Tram Ride

I loved to ride upon the tram
Seats swayed and bounced with me sat on them
That lovely sound *clickity clack*
As it raced along the track
The conductor with his peaked cap
Shouts, 'Move along inside, mind your back'
With his swaying, graceful walk
Fills the journey with his talk
Moves up and down inside the car
Squeezing past people, hanging onto the bar
'Anymore fares please,' he does cry
Hold your money out, don't be shy
One *ding* on the bell to stop
Two *dings* on the bell to go
The driver with his hand on the dead man's handle
Lurched and swayed like a flame on a candle
Though its journey is at an end
I mourn its passing, like a friend
I see again in my mind's eye
The last tram go rattling by.

William J Jones

OBSERVATION

I saw a child run wild and free
Wild and free, beside the sea
I saw a man with quiet gaze
Try to pierce the distant haze
I saw a woman, calm and proud
Feel the wind, observe the cloud
Call to man and child aloud
I saw a boat with sails full spread
Race the seagulls overhead
I saw the moon, remote, serene
Silvering waves and sands so clean
I saw the night remove all trace
Of sight of boat, of human race.

June Davies

OTHERWISE

In nobody's world,
I'm a tumble-down child,
How can I be, so wild?
I've fathomed sake, that caused me, ill will,
Now not be, mistake,
If I thought it, fulfil,
I cannot see, all that's good, in this world,
Having a chip, axe to grind,
I've no place, as home,
Where I could, but roam,
My thoughts, oft in mind, were unkind,
Have had, a hard life,
And am glad, there's only one,
Those brickbats, in plenty, galore,
I've looked round, my stead,
With a thought, oft in dread,
The new things, in life, I'll explore,
There isn't so much, to be done,
For fortune not called, to my door,
It hasn't been gentle, to me, in this life,
With hard times, aplenty,
Through trouble, and strife,
Did know my mum, when I was small,
My dad, I hardly saw,
They shouted and fought, had their blows,
Someone, might call it, a draw,
It's all I've seen, through my, whole life,
And has made me, what I am,
Not caring whether, things were right,
Each day, was like, grand slam.

Hugh Campbell

Yellow Rose

You passed to me a yellow rose
That evening in the city square,
A statue cast a shadow
On this moment that we share.

The seller smiled and looked at me.
You laughed at him and asked for one;
Affronted by his fortune's loss
He turned, complained, was gone.

You told me of the nascent night
Your father stole your mother's rose,
The monuments bore witness
To the resting place he chose.

That sign of loss now love's reward
With memories made so softly then.
My yellow rose remains intact
And love clings to its stem.

Indy Clark

CATNAP

Beneath my hedge there slept a cat
I saw it as I drew the blind
Perhaps still chasing mouse or rat
It slumbered on, so tightly curled.
All morning as the sun crept round
And touched its fur with golden warmth
It did not stir, but sleeping sound
And hedged securely, safely dreamed
And then, was gone.

M E A Lloyd

A Time For Rhyme

My friend, I am not adverse
To poems written in free verse,
But I prefer the rhythm of rhyme
To paint the pictures in my mind.
Childhood poems give such pleasure
Remembering, I always treasure
Words in waltz or marching time
That linger in my memory
Enchanted with such grammary.

Muriel Berry

RAINDROPS

Waking up in the morning to the
Raindrops falling on the roof.
We really need this water,
And now we have the proof.
The farmers will be happy;
They have sown their seed.
Whilst the ducks swim on the river,
They will enjoy their splash indeed.
Things will look and smell so fresh;
The flowers will now lift their heads,
I watch the robin take a bath;
His breast looks a brilliant red.
The children like to wear their boots
As they splash along their homeward route.
Suddenly I look up in the sky
The dark clouds are passing by.
A rainbow emerges across the screen.
Let's thank God for nature, for the natural things we see,
Listening to the church bells ring
Hearing the beauty as the birds sing.

Aves Swanson

THE CAMEL

Daddy was very cross this morning
And gave the table quite a thump,
Mummy said when he had gone,
Your daddy's got the hump.

That puzzled me a bit because
I thought a hump was on a camel,
And my daddy looks nothing like
That great big hairy mammal.

They tell me that a camel can
Go eight days without a drink,
So I'm sure my daddy's not a camel,
I don't even have to think.

Each night when he comes home,
After a long hard day at work,
His first action is a duty,
I've never seen him shirk.

He goes to the big old sideboard,
And there straight up he is stood,
And pours himself some medicine;
It seems to do a power of good.

At least, medicine is what he said,
When I asked him what was its name,
Though I think it was gin and tonic.
I can see through his little game.

Robert H Quin

THERE WAS A TIME

There was a time when anticipation was a magic word,
giving rise to excitement before the event occurred.
Seeing candyfloss twirling around its stick in the machine,
anticipating that first sweet taste, oh what a dream.

But nowadays it seems, most things are done in haste,
allowing no time for magic - what a waste.
As we journey through life there are many lessons to learn,
like, it isn't always about getting there first, but taking your turn.

That way you will be able to remember where you have been,
and recall the feeling of pleasure about things you have seen.
The friendships you make will always be there,
because you took time to show how you really do care.

Then there is the importance of not letting today become yesterday,
without a backward glance,
because you don't want to miss a moment of taking every chance.
To realise what a wonderful feeling it would be,
to say, 'yes there was a time, and it belonged to me'.

B Lamus

WISHING

It's frosty, but sunny,
I wish I had the money
To get away from this place
And feel the sun on my face.

Alas, my disability stops me going
Too far away from home,
So I'll sit in the garden
And hope I don't look like a gnome.

No, I don't have a fishing rod,
Nor do I sit at the edge of a pool,
I just sit on the garden seat
And I'm hoping I don't look like a fool.

I still have a lot to be grateful for,
My family is very caring.
They look after so well
And make sure I don't do anything daring.

Like wanting to climb Mount Everest,
Even though I'd stop for a rest.
Go hot air ballooning,
Or maybe start crooning?

My voice may sound like a foghorn,
But that's the one I was born with.
So I sit here on my garden seat,
Ah! This is the place you can't beat.

Margaret Rose

The Old Orkney Chair

I have travelled round the world
I have seen many a land.
But my heart has always been at home
In the house on the strand.
Oh, my dear Orkney home
I would dream I was there
I could see my dear mother
On the old Orkney chair.

She would keep the house so tidy
Just like a new pin
When strangers came to the door
She would invite them in.
She would clean all the brasses
She would polish them with care
Then she would have forty winks
On the old Orkney chair.

I would come home from school
Thinking - what is for tea?
I would run then I'd stumble
I would fall and hurt my knee.
I would limp home to Mother
For I knew she'd be there.
She'd kiss me then hug me
On the old Orkney chair.

Those years have long gone
Now Mother has passed away.
But, I know she'll protect me
As I journey through each day.
The house is now empty
The kitchen is now bare
Yet, I still see my mother
On the old Orkney chair.

Hamish M Davidson

THE MAN IN THE MOON

The man in the moon is not in sight,
I have not seen him for a while;
And I miss that craggy countenance,
That enigmatic smile.

We've been friends for near a lifetime,
The man in the moon and I,
Since as a boy I waved to him
In a clear and moonlit sky.

But my sight is growing dimmer,
And the years are drawing on;
But I know he will be looking down
For many moons after I am gone.

He has been lost a lifetime so it seems
To the children of today . . . I fear
They do not know the simple joys
That kept us happy yesteryear.

They have PC web sites to explore,
Discos confused by sound and light,
And video tapes of every type
To sit and watch into the night.

They have never read Hans Anderson,
Nor pursued the Brothers Grimm;
And Aesop, 'Who's is he?' they ask,
'We have never heard of him'.

When I recount to them the treasures
And the simple joys they may be missing,
They smile and whisper each to each,
'He is just an old man, reminiscing'.

Thomas R Slater

NEED TO RHYME

Some very modern people
Think rhyming poetry's old hat,
As someone who loves words and verse
I cannot agree with that,
How lovely to feel the flow
And find the words to rhyme,
Looking in the dictionary
Is what often takes the time.

To try to tell a story
About who, or what or where,
Making words fit together
For poetry readers to share,
So many fabulous subjects
In verses short and long,
We need more clever people
To put rhyming back where it belongs.

Some modern stuff is pleasant
But not my cup of tea,
Give me a good old fashioned verse
As pleased as punch I'd be,
The new wave is more complex
And not always understood,
We've had some brilliant rhymers
Whose work is oh so good.

So come on let's get rhyming
Try to bring it to the fore,
Show there's a space for both sorts
Enjoy it, I you implore,
So I've had a go with a few lines
See what sort of job I'd make,
I will try to get one published
Just for rhyming's sake.

Win Barton

A BUTTERFLY FLIES

No one denies
A butterfly flies
With a zigzag fluttering flight
Though often now knowing
Which way it's going
It's certainly a splendid sight
But when it's not flying
Maybe it's trying
To devise a way to fly straight
Only to find
That it was designed
Always to deviate.

So it's not surprising
When suddenly rising
Veering to the left and the right
The way a butterfly flies
Seems to hypnotise
With its fluttering flight of delight.

Cecil J Lewis

HAPPY BIRTHDAY, MUM

I know it makes you want to laugh
When I run off as you say, 'bath'.
I get so tatty, rough and scruffy
You make me clean and neat and fluffy
You do your best - I know you try
To keep the soap out of each eye.
It's fun when we all chase my bone
And when I bark to hear the phone.
Then, when I want to be let out
For 'wees' and things - or sniff about
I know you love me - as does Dad
Although it makes him rather mad
At mealtimes when he sits there stuffing
I play him up with constant wuffing.
I'm pretty good - patient and quiet
And always eat my daily diet,
Shame the good Lord made me dumb
Because - I'd like to tell you Mum
I love you in my doggy way
Not only now - but every day.
So thank you Mum for the care and fun
You've given to your canine son.
Dad loves you too when you don't nag
Shame he has no tail to wag.

Eric E Webb

LIFE OVER

A child is born, first breath, first cries
From now on a new life until she dies
Helpless, innocent, on mother she depends
Demanding all time (when does this end?)

Taking those first steps, a tumble, a cry
We cherish those days (which soon passes by)
School days are here, how quickly they grow
They become independent (everything they know)

Exams and study, qualifications to achieve
Then sad farewells, as education they leave
Into the real world of earning and living
Learning to survive by taking and giving

They have their own life, they go their own way
Often no contact . . . then they're here to stay
So life still goes on repeating the start
At first they make your arms ache . . . then later your heart.

Jo Hodson

Cat's Breakfast

A furry insistence dances about in my way,
For the cat intends to eradicate every perception
Except his needs; to take part in a tragic play
As a starving waif, big-eyed, who has no recollection

Of when he ate last, and is now at the point of death
Unless fed. I open a tin labelled salmon and trout.
He merely sniffs at the plate, then in the next breath
He stalks to the door and urgently asks to go out.

How strange the bare scent of food can allay such sorrow!
Puss's acting won't fool me again - at least till tomorrow.

S R Hawk'sbee

Ullswater Lament

Open your throttles Raven,
Open them wide and roar,
So speed your way to Pooley Bridge
But I'll be on board no more.

Two years ago my love and I
You bore across Ullswater,
But now she's gone; we'll sail no more,
And so's my son and daughter.

A lonely man stands on the quay,
Glenridding lies behind,
A car park and some sailing boats,
A river to remind.

Like Raven, so my love's sailed on,
Just ripples on the shore
Remind me that she once was here
But I'll be on board no more, no more,
I'll be on board no more.

John Belcher

BEAUTIFUL TIMES

Do you remember the time,
that you spilt the red wine,
and we decided to stay in bed,
and the time on the train,
when it started to rain,
just a paper to cover your head,

Do you remember the nights,
when we turned down the lights,
and spent evenings all huddled in love,
or the time in the park,
it was just after dark,
the stars surrounded the moon up above,

Those were beautiful times,
ones that I'll treasure,
and now captured in rhyme,
forever and ever,

Do you remember my face,
when you dressed up in lace,
and then went out to dance on the lawn,
or the lake in the mist,
where we stood there and kissed,
and didn't get home until after dawn,

Do you remember your look,
when I bought you that book,
of the poet you said you once knew,
and you read out the song,
that you said would belong,
in our hearts, between me and you.

Chris Silvester

HOME FROM GREECE

Bright vacationer lands regress to dream,
When dark rain asserts its despondent hold,
Returning to a claustrophobic scene,
An unwilling 'black sheep' enters the fold.

My aspirations reached their finest hour
In air nebulous with incessant sun,
But now ambition's wraith, repressed and sour,
Lies fetid in a vacuum bled of fun.

Don't ask me in my present cold remorse,
What dreams I realised in those foreign nights:
I danced with strangers, rode a Greek's black horse:
Played the satyr in dionysic rites.

My dreaded anathema is the pain
Of stepping down from Heaven's heady heights,
To fasten inhibition's heavy chain
With reason's lock around taboo delights.

Dave Austin

A Beautiful Life

When you came into the world
You touched my heart
A whole new being unfurled
And turned into such a sweetheart

Now that you've reached sixteen
I stand back and look at you
I could not of foreseen
This bright energetic young girl that turned out to be you

I hope you stay the same
Fun, loving and kind
As you go on to play life's game
And take your place in womankind

Whatever you choose to do
You'll always have a place in my heart
No matter what becomes of you
I will always be proud to be your aunt.

P Taylor

PHASE DAYS

Have you ever thought back
on the way that you looked.
The stages you went through and fashions you cooked.
Your parents' displeasure that you became the pop star,
your idol, you would look the same.
Eighties teen, and era of punk,
your father's heart,
that you had sunk.
Hair dye on your mother's towels.
The family dog looks and growls,
the arguments were thick and fast.
I didn't see why,
The phase just past.
By time I'd hit working age
I'd reached a totally different stage.

A A Brown

Addict's Spirits

You desperately love it
you need it, you're an addict.
What you'll do to have it
nobody can predict.

For money, for power,
to Hell he is going.
He rapes ever flower
to get black heroin.

His box full of masks
for each situation.
But one of them asks
bold, emergent question.

How could you do that?
To cause so many tears?
It's name is Regret,
hasn't been used for years.

He says, 'I'm the best!'
but he knows it's just a lie.
He opens his chest
that his spirits can fly.

Into the cursed land
his spirits fly faster.
They burn glass from sand
as commands their master.

Some innocent souls
spirits hurry to kill,
his hungry pack howls,
their anger makes them ill.

On the whole world his anger rains
from his mighty empire
into sick and old Earth's veins
he strikes his teeth like a vampire.

Ivan Daniš

FORTY DRINKS

Oh wake me up from slumbers
There's a badge on my lapel
Drinks by countless numbers
And now I feel unwell.

My mobile phone's erratic
I can't ring my dear wife
Must be all that static
Story of my life!

A friendly tap on shoulder
'You've missed your station mate!'
At Ingatestone it's colder
No taxis after eight.

I did get home for dinner
'It's in the oven - burnt!'
At party time a sinner
Lessons have been learnt!

Steve Glason

MYSTERY WOMAN

Look at her eyes shining bright,
They really make a comforting sight.

Her musical voice ringing out to the stars,
All the way to Venus and Mars.

She's warm, soft and very funny,
She also likes to spend her money.

She is brilliant and kind,
She has an intelligent mind.

This person is my mum,
She can't make a bun.

But I love her,
Cos she is my mum.

Carrie Thorpe (12)

ANCHOR BOOKS
SUBMISSIONS INVITED
SOMETHING FOR EVERYONE

ANCHOR BOOKS GEN - Any subject, light-hearted clean fun, nothing unprintable please.

THE OPPOSITE SEX - Have your say on the opposite gender. Do they drive you mad or can we co-exist in harmony?

THE NATURAL WORLD - Are we destroying the world around us? What should we do to preserve the beauty and the future of our planet - you decide!

All poems no longer than 30 lines.
Always welcome! No fee!
Plus cash prizes to be won!

Mark your envelope (eg *The Natural World*)
And send to:
Anchor Books
Remus House, Coltsfoot Drive
Peterborough, PE2 9JX

OVER £10,000 IN POETRY PRIZES TO BE WON!

Send an SAE for details on our New Year 2003 competition!